# HAPPINESS RECLAIMED

How I Heal & Thrive in This Crazy World
(And How You Can Too)

Carol Diane

*Important Warning and Disclaimer*

The information provided in this book is for general knowledge and educational purposes only, reflects the author's personal experience and recollection thereof, and does NOT constitute medical advice or other professional advice. Always seek the advice of a physician, other qualified healthcare provider, or other suitable professional for any questions or concerns you may have on any topic. Never disregard medical advice or delay in seeking it because of something you have read in this book. The author and publisher do not make any warranties or representations, express or implied, about the suitability or reliability of the information for any particular purpose. The author and publisher disclaim all liability for any errors or omissions in the book, and for any consequences arising from the use or reliance on the information contained herein. Any reliance on the information in this book is at the reader's own risk. Therefore, the publisher and author are not liable for any personal injury or damage arising from any improper application or a failure of the reader to seek correct medical or other professional advice. Drugs used for a different condition or purpose than the one for which they were originally granted a license are known as "off-label." The U.S. Food and Drug Administration has not approved the use of "off-label" drugs for the treatment of cancer. Only you and your doctor can decide what is right for any health condition or concern you may have.

Copyright © 2025 Carol Diane
ISBN: 978-1-943627-06-6

All rights reserved. No part of this publication may be reproduced, distributed, or transmitted in any form or by any means, including photocopying, recording, or other electronic or mechanical methods, without the prior written permission of the publisher, except in the case of brief quotations with proper attribution, and other non-commercial uses permitted by copyright law. For permission requests, contact Carol Diane at HappinessReclaimed.com.

This book is dedicated to Josh.
Of all the people who helped me survive,
he belongs at the top of the list.

# *Table of Contents*

| | |
|---|---|
| 1. What If… | 7 |
| 2. Setting a Healthy Framework | 9 |
| 3. Welcome to My World | 12 |
| **Mind** | **15** |
| 4. A Love for Learning | 17 |
| 5. Discipline and the United Front | 19 |
| 6. Financial Maturity | 25 |
| 7. Freedom of Thought | 27 |
| 8. Breaking Old Chains | 33 |
| 9. Deeper into My Past | 46 |
| 10. The Road Runner | 49 |
| 11. Enticement, Deception, Betrayal | 55 |
| 12. Treasuring Life | 64 |
| 13. Obstacles to Personal Growth, Perhaps | 70 |
| **Body** | **85** |
| 14. The Origin of My Holistic Approach | 87 |
| 15. The Next Three Decades | 93 |
| 16. The First Major Crisis | 99 |
| 17. From Eye Problems to Cancer | 112 |
| 18. Cancer Factors? | 120 |
| 19. Cancer—State #1 | 138 |
| 20. Cancer—State #2 | 167 |
| 21. Cancer—State #3 | 177 |
| 22. Cancer—State #4 | 182 |
| **Spirit** | **189** |
| 23. Basic Concepts | 191 |
| 24. The Stumbling Block of Divinity | 206 |
| 25. Supernatural Experiences | 213 |
| **Final Thoughts** | **223** |
| **Notes** | **229** |

# 1
## What If…

…we stopped for a moment, took a breath, looked at our problems, and said,

> "No! We're not doing this anymore! We're going to see BEYOND the problem and do ONE simple thing that creates instant change."

Not 100% change! But instant change in one area of life—whichever priority we choose! Then we keep walking down that NEW road, accumulating more and more success. And then the ripple effect kicks in. One life touches a life that touches a life that touches a life.

Your life transformed. Your community transformed. A whole nation transformed!

That's what Happiness Reclaimed is all about. I hope you'll join me.

**Important Note:** What follows is the story of how I got to this point—the point where I finally said, in so many different ways at different times in my life, "No! I'm not doing this anymore!"

We'll cover different kinds of adversity—two "incurable" diseases, emotional and psychological abuse, sexual abuse, loneliness, and more. We'll cover the challenges we all face in science, medicine, politics, and human nature. But most importantly, we'll see how some of the worst things in life become the greatest blessings! We have the power to turn the world upside down!

Along the way, if my story begins to feel too heavy for you, I encourage you to go to the Powerful Life Strategies at my website HappinessReclaimed.com, pick the strategy that's a priority for you, and start changing your life. Honor your own individual journey. I will meet you wherever you are!

# 2

# Setting a Healthy Framework

Hi there! I'm so glad you're here! Let's begin by highlighting what some of us call "The Law of Healthy Boundaries." Starting here will help you benefit from this book and avoid misinterpretation and bad results. I imagine everyone has heard this word "boundaries." Let's focus on the core essence of the concept—the idea that there's a boundary or healthy separation between one person and all other individuals. Therefore, all human beings have the right and responsibility to think for themselves. This idea helps form the very core of human dignity, respect, and freedom.

I am determined to show my readers that respect, so these ideas follow:

**At no time am I telling anyone what to do in a specific situation.** Only you can decide what is right for you, regardless of whether you're pondering a human relationship issue, a health issue, or a spiritual issue. Although I share health information, psychological information, and more, I can only share what I myself have discovered. Not only is that body of information extremely limited, but also, as you'll learn, it's often unclear what is actually true.

Even in science, research studies often produce conflicting results, and even when a consensus among scientists has been reached, that consensus can shift over time—what was once declared true might later be labeled as false, and vice versa. Or something might not be considered completely false, but overly simplistic. And what's more, the SPEED of this change seems to be increasing due to technological advances. Also, each human being has a unique combination of genes, biochemical conditions that turn those genes on or off, and variations in diet, microbiome, exercise, sleep quality, environmental exposure, thought patterns, and more.

Therefore, the information provided in this book is for general knowledge and educational purposes only and does NOT constitute medical advice or other professional advice. Always seek the advice of a physician, other qualified healthcare provider, or other suitable professional for any questions or concerns you may have on any topic. My publisher and I do not make any warranties or representations, express or implied, about the suitability or reliability of the information for any particular purpose, and we disclaim all liability for any errors or omissions in the book, and for any consequences arising from the use or reliance on the information contained herein. Any reliance on the information in this book is at the reader's own risk. In all three areas—mind, body, spirit—only YOU can decide what is right for you.

**Freedom of thought and speech are sacred rights that benefit us all.** Any religious reference or socio-political opinion or medical opinion that I offer should be taken in context as my personal opinion, and we should trust all people to exercise their right and responsibility to think for themselves. We don't have to agree with one another. Censorship destroys the rights of all of us, and it can even put our lives in jeopardy.

**In EVERY sentence, I am speaking only for myself with a "General I-Statement."** It would be ridiculously repetitive if I used the phrase "I think" or "I believe" or "in my opinion" in every sentence, but that's how I'd like you to receive my entire communication, and every sentence should be received as saying "generally speaking," unless I specify otherwise. (Please see Powerful Strategy #1 on my website to better understand General I-Statements.)

In fact, I am speaking only for myself even if I offer what SOUNDS LIKE advice: To use an extreme example, if I say, "I think your life would be better if you ate chocolate ice cream," that is just an opinion, and others have the responsibility to think for themselves, and perhaps choose to say "No, thanks." What's more, they can reject an idea without elevating their stress hormones!

**Here is a path to freedom for us all**—freedom from unnecessary stress as we learn to be at peace with the individuality of others! By truly accepting the rights of others, we will be helping OURSELVES most of all! This is because, as animosity starts to flow **out of us**, poison has already begun the damage **inside of us**.

We are all separate individuals, and we must stand strong to protect everyone's right to be a separate individual. Thank you for understanding and standing up to protect the rights of all of us! And so, with that healthy framework established, let's begin.

# 3

# Welcome to My World

At this point in my life, just about the only thing I know for sure is I don't know much for sure. But I could be wrong about that!

**ON THE ONE HAND, I've learned to feel grateful for this uncertainty and self-doubt**—which I did not invite but received as a gift through devastating betrayals and disappointments—because it seems the last thing we need in this world is more controlling know-it-alls who consider their opinions infallible, rush to judgment about you, or get annoyed if you dare to have a different opinion. Right? I know the pain and psychological damage that comes from being around people like that. Maybe you do too. So I definitely don't want to be like that.

I've heard it said, "The secret of life is to remember you could be wrong, and your goal in life is to be less wrong." Yeah! That's what I'm talking about! That's what I think of as humility. Always eager to learn, to grow, to improve. Not putting too much faith in our own thoughts, feelings, or perceptions. I love the saying, "Who are the most objective people? The people who know they're NOT objective!" Amen!

I'm not saying we shouldn't have deeply held beliefs. I'm just saying none of us is God and a little bit of uncertainty and humility is a good thing. We can always learn something new or understand something more deeply. I'll be blunt: We should not be stubborn, ignorant fools. If we do, people may tolerate us, but secretly, they sure won't like us. So maybe I don't know much of anything, and I sincerely mean that. Five, ten, or twenty years from now, how will my beliefs and attitudes be different?

**BUT ON THE OTHER HAND, I'm thinking maybe I've stumbled upon a collection of important truths that could save your life—or save the QUALITY of your life.** Maybe by sharing these ideas with you, I can fully redeem all my years of suffering. By that I mean, maybe I didn't go through all this just for my own education and spiritual growth. Maybe I'm meant to help others. You get to be the judge of that.

**I believe my job is to tell you what I've experienced, what I've observed by knowing other people, and what I've come to believe. Then you can do your own research and decide what you wish to believe and what works for you as a unique individual.**

**I'm also writing this book with a SECOND GOAL in mind:** I've decided it's time to leave my painful past in the dustbin of history. The research scientists and ancient scriptures agree: We benefit from dwelling on things that are lovely, admirable, praiseworthy. We can learn from the past and should recognize evil when it confronts us today, but we shouldn't remain stuck in the past—nor should we worry about the future. Now that I've been fighting off stage-four cancer, I understand the cost of dwelling in the past, worrying about the future, and agonizing over my present problems. I can't afford those stress hormones!

**BUT AT THE SAME TIME,** I am constantly meeting people who need to know my background for one reason or another. So this book can fill that need and become my final telling of that story. After this, I will discuss only the positive: What did I learn? How did I survive? How can we all move forward together?

So here goes. I will tell you WHAT I can in the WAY that I can. I pray you find it helpful. But get ready. It may be a rough ride. You may not want to hear certain parts. You might want to blame me or dismiss me as "crazy." You wouldn't be the first! But read on and I think you'll realize you don't want to be one of them.

If you don't get anything else from this book, at least learn the lesson I began with: If we all can drop our pride, take on a little humility, quiet and slow down our emotional reactions, and open our minds, we might just learn something new, something that makes our lives better, or helps the ones we love. And if this book is just like all the others you've read, what good is it?

*Mind*

# 4
# A Love for Learning

I grew up in a middle-class family that was wonderful in so many ways. Too many to list, actually! My parents were representative examples of the American Dream as we understood it in post-WWII America. In that single generation, they made the transition from struggling in poverty during the Great Depression to enjoying middle-class affluence in the 1950s and beyond.

They came from a long line of peasants, farmers, and factory workers, none of whom had much education. But thanks to my father's service during the war, the G.I. Bill, and my father's hard work, we kids grew up in a nice home with parents who emphasized achievement and the value of a good education. They gifted me with a love for learning—not just by expecting me to do my best in school, but also by modeling hard work, self-sacrifice, delay of gratification, and curiosity.

My father was a chemist, and discussions around the dinner table were inevitably filled with logical thought and careful analysis. One evening, when I was in fifth grade, I told my family that my teacher had horrified us by saying the protein content on the ketchup bottle label indicated smashed bugs in the tomatoes!

My father scoffed and said, "Where did the bugs get THEIR protein?"

See what I mean? Learning to question what people tell you is a good thing. And learning to think is absolutely essential. Don't let anyone dumb you down or dumb down your children or grandchildren. And don't let people intimidate you into silence. Sincere questions are for the benefit of all—they aren't disrespectful. They might even save your life one day, or the life of someone you love. We'll encounter this theme a few more times as we go along!

# 5

# Discipline and the United Front

My parents also gave me the deep sense of SECURITY and RESPECT that comes from discipline and sticking together as a united front. **I suspect the psychological and spiritual benefit of the parental united front is not properly appreciated in today's culture.**

When it came to discipline, I knew how I was expected to behave, and I knew I did not want to violate those rules. If I did, watch out! Yes, there was an element of fear, but it's a healthy fear, I think. And experts will tell you a child who grows up in a permissive environment feels unloved and insecure: *Where are the boundaries? Does anyone care enough to enforce boundaries?*

I did not have to have those devastating thoughts and I pity children who did. Parents who try to be the buddy are not helping their children, but damaging them. So when parents bring that first baby home, I believe it's important to leave behind all those teenage yearnings for popularity. Step up to your call of duty: Your job is to lay down any unhealthy need for approval and do what's best for your child. Accept the idea that you may never be a buddy. You will never be "cool." Then you will be free to do right by your child.

And get ready for some manipulation from your children. They will try. I remember years later, when I was enforcing some boundary with MY daughters, one of them—probably four years old—would yell from her time-out chair, "I'm never having mommy time with you again!"

"Mommy time" was our name for one-on-one quality time. When she made that threat, I probably let her know in a calm voice that I thought that would be sad, or I might have remained silent, but I think she figured out the threat wasn't moving me. I wouldn't lose sleep over that. After a few more times, those attempts at manipulation ended. She has brought that up and laughed about it in more recent years.

And when I was a kid, like every other kid, I had to test those boundaries. When I was two or three, I was with my father as he was rummaging through his toolbox, laying out tools to find the one he wanted. I had reached for the tools and he told me not to touch. Of course I had to try again. I got spanked for that and cried hard. Maybe today we would prefer he had put me in a time-out chair rather than angrily spanking me, but at least I learned to obey that day.

For me, after that day, painful episodes of discipline were rare. I obeyed the rules I knew. But sometimes I had a new lesson to learn. When I was in junior high, my plan one Halloween was to trick-or-treat through my neighborhood with one set of friends, then make my way across town to another friend's house—let's say her name was Donna. Well, I was enjoying my time with the first set of kids, and I just blew off Donna, never bothered to show up. She called my house to inquire, of course. So my mom knew about it before I got home. When I did come home, hoo-wee! Did I ever get chewed out! It was an angry lecture about considering the feelings of others. That really stung, and I remember feeling victimized and unloved. But I'll tell you what: I learned that day to think about other people's feelings, and I thank God my mother let me have it. I needed that and I was a better person for it. I think I truly changed that day. Thanks, Mom!

This parental discipline goes haywire if parents can't stand united, but my parents remained a united front. There was no subsequent message from my dad that could be construed as: "Carol, we know your mother can be difficult. I'm the sympathetic good guy."

There was no discussion at all, and even if there had been, there would have been no use of the word "we," referring to my father and me discussing my mother behind her back. Likewise, I never received such messages from my mother about my father.

Some counselors call those toxic manipulations "parental alienation." In custody battles, that phrase might have a specific legal definition, but even within an ongoing marriage, parental alienation can occur, and it really screws up the kids, regardless of their age. The parent who does that is teaching children to be two-faced, dishonest, secretive, disloyal, and manipulative, rather than teaching them to handle conflict in a mature, assertive, Godly way.

What drives a parent to do that? Well, I can offer a few theories. Sometimes divisive parents are themselves two-faced, dishonest, secretive, disloyal, and manipulative, and those traits are transmitted from one generation to the next in precisely this way. Can you see how a secretive, us-against-him or us-against-her conversation leads to the fulfillment of every one of those adjectives? Alternatively, divisive parents might lack that maturity I mentioned earlier. Maybe growing up, they felt like a "loser" socially, and they couldn't shake that teenage craving for popularity. So undermining one's spouse could be a desperate reach for popularity. Or sometimes jealousy and anger drive vengeful behavior. Parental alienation happens more than you might think. Ask any experienced marriage-and-family counselor.

A quick note of caution here: The victimized parent complaining about parental alienation is NOT another example of parental alienation, but is it helpful to speak about this problem directly to the children, even when they're young adults?

Well, that's a separate issue. That can be counterproductive. Sometimes the best thing is to remain silent and pray the kids shake their brainwashing and see the truth. For that to occur, the kids will need some maturity and spiritual discernment. Even if they're now adults, the truth of how they were manipulated might be too hard to face. It's no fun realizing you've been taught toxic patterns from the time you were young. It's no fun losing respect for the divisive parent after being taught for years to disrespect the victimized parent. Talk about a cataclysmic paradigm shift! Talk about your whole world crashing down! Denial might be much more comfortable, especially if the children know THEY were disrespectful toward that parent. Now we're throwing guilt and shame into the mix, so it's even harder to face the ugly truth! Guilt and shame drive ANY kind of scapegoating, and parental alienation is just one subcategory of scapegoating.

There are, I think, at least two essential keys to grown children coming out of denial and realizing what has occurred:

1. They need to understand the whole situation is not their fault. They were just children when the whole thing began and could not have known what healthy parenting should look like. They never asked for all the drama! THEY ARE VICTIMS TOO!

2. At the same time, paradoxically, they need to be in a place spiritually where they really can look at their own faults and mistakes, see the dark side of human nature which we all possess. As time passed, their behavior HAD to conflict more and more with societal norms for what is polite, loving, generous, and kind. As they grew older, their minds must have gradually become conscious of the fact that their treatment of that parent was not right. This contradiction between conscience and behavior is called "cognitive dissonance." It's an uncomfortable feeling for all human beings. So a common way to resolve the dissonance is to decide that parent DESERVES rude or uncaring behavior. There must be something so terrible about this parent that he or she deserves the rudeness, excluding, shunning, gossiping, blaming, and perhaps even physical violence or theft.

These two points may seem contradictory. After all, that's one definition of "paradox." But that's because life is a moving target, not one snapshot in time. As time goes by, things evolve, and the cognitive dissonance naturally grows. A guilty conscience, no matter how deeply buried, no matter how much it is denied, will not only rot a person's soul, but will also rot a person's physical and emotional health. Various health conditions such as gut issues, pain, cancer, and more, and various psychological issues such as chronic anxiety, obsessive-compulsive tendencies, hypochondria, ALL of these can be caused to some degree by the anxious awareness deep down that something is not right. The human body is not designed to carry such constant stress.

If those children grow up to be parents themselves, they'll probably have more sympathy for parental roles, and a clearer vision of how parents should be treated. We all tend to have greater sympathy when a social problem hits us personally. But our media-driven culture has been moving AGAINST respect for parents for decades now, undermining parental authority. I could name numerous TV shows, movies, and hit songs that have served that purpose. But I won't bother. I will, however, tell you a brief story that shows how pervasive this effort has been.

When one of my daughters turned twelve and I took her to the pediatrician for the required physical, they handed her a booklet labeled as advice "for nine- to twelve-year-olds." As I recall, one section was discussing illegal drugs and sexual activity, and it said something like this: When you were young, you parroted the opinions of your parents, but now you are old enough to make up your own mind.

*Whaaaaat? You're telling me children 12 and younger are ready to make a wise decision about sexual activity and illegal drugs? I wasn't capable of making a wise decision about that even at 17 and beyond! (Something I deeply regret now that I know more.)*

Notice the subtle—or not so subtle—effort to encourage children to reject parental wisdom and advice. Of course, that was decades ago. Now our culture has descended to a darker depth. It's time to turn this around, folks. Ah, modern-day family life! Isn't it fun? But by the time you finish this book, you'll have some new attitudes and strategies at your disposal.

# 6

# Financial Maturity

My parents also modeled handling money wisely. We kids were neither deprived nor spoiled—we were in that perfect middle zone. Likewise, my parents controlled their spending on themselves. They bought things for themselves but also watched their budget carefully. No out-of-control spending here!

Children benefit tremendously from seeing their parents exercise such self-control. Many habits and values are "caught" more than they are taught. In other words, we often pick up habits and values by observing our parents, rather than through explicit instruction.

I think children benefit from their parents' financial maturity in at least two ways. First, as I've suggested, they learn to control their own future spending by "catching" those values from their parents. Minimizing financial stress is key for successful adulthood and a happy marriage, especially because arguments over money are a common factor in divorce.

A second benefit occurs when children learn to accept the word "no." They learn the broader truth that they can't have everything they want in life. I think this is another underrated value in today's culture—our ability to remain happy and content even when things don't go our way. We're also talking about generosity and sharing—taking turns with our spouse regarding whose desire gets satisfied with the next purchase. I've seen marriages in which one partner expects to have every material want satisfied, and I've seen the financial and emotional stress that follows. But my parents found that marvelous middle zone—being both disciplined in their spending AND reasonably generous to one another and us kids.

Besides being the main breadwinner, my dad's other financial contribution was being a fanatical do-it-yourselfer to save money. There wasn't much he couldn't design, build, or fix. He truly was an inspiration! My mom also was frugal. Although she left childhood with a sense of shame over being poor and a passion for stylish clothing and home decor, she still exercised self-control in her spending.

I never experienced that shame, so I was never as concerned about my appearance. I wasn't sloppy—I'm sure my mom had a positive influence on me—but I just wasn't as interested as she was, and I have almost always disliked clothes shopping. This was never an issue between us as far as I knew. We respected each other's differences. And that's a good thing.

# 7
# Freedom of Thought

Respecting differences was not as easy for my father. With that brilliant intellect, he was prone to strong opinions. And it seems he carried anger from having an abusive father and a mother who favored his brother. For all I know, there could have been additional factors. Although he could be quite jovial at times, he also could come across as not only domineering, but also critical and angry. Many times, I went to my room and cried over the way I was treated.

For example, one day I was slicing a tomato. Apparently I wasn't doing it right. My father angrily grabbed the knife from me and said, "Here, let ME do it!" I don't recall struggling with that tomato. I don't know what the problem could have been. I was just a kid.

Overall, I grew up expecting criticism, and knowing my opinions had better match his or an angry retort might come my way. In a raised voice, he would fiercely or even angrily let me know I was wrong. Somehow, in some way, I was wrong. Being the baby of the family and the unwanted third child didn't help. We babies of the family can experience being treated as though we don't know much. And unwanted children can sometimes be scapegoated.

I imagine you're starting to see how I developed that uncertainty and humility I talked about. But you know, I sincerely meant it when I said I see those traits as gifts.

**Some of the greatest gifts in life come from adversity!**

Don't believe me? Think that's just a rationalization? Sick of platitudes like that? Well, I sometimes feel annoyed by platitudes too. Of course it hurt terribly to be regularly told I was wrong, even when I was right. I know what that and his anger did to my sense of self-worth, and it's a long road of recovery, which I am still on. But get a load of this: Now I hear from researchers there's tremendous value in maintaining this more humble and open mindset!

Researchers say people with this trait tend to be more curious and creative, and they see the world more accurately! They think the most important thing is figuring out what's true. They don't mind finding out they're wrong because THEIR SELF-WORTH IS NO LONGER TIED TO BEING RIGHT. Instead, they see learning they're wrong as making progress on the journey toward truth. It's actually an interesting or even exciting discovery! And changing their mind isn't viewed as weakness—it's personal strength. As a result of this mindset, they welcome open discussion and wish everyone could participate in a healthy, happy way.

When I heard about this research, I realized it describes me, and it now helps me understand some of my deepest heartaches. I have felt isolated and lonely when surrounded by people who couldn't likewise be open-minded and curious. I couldn't explore the world with them! And I have sometimes been hurt by close-mindedness.

**And I realize I'm not alone in my pain! I think this close-mindedness is now at epidemic proportions, and many of us are suffering without fully realizing what the problem is, or that it doesn't have to be this way!**

Some of us live in constant fear of negative judgment if we would dare to reveal our authentic selves. Others fear being wrong. Some get annoyed if you innocently ask a question they don't know how to answer. Their egos are so fragile that the rest of us might react by walking on eggshells to keep the peace. Some are jealously guarding their positions, thinking they need to stay "safe" from diverse views. I don't want to be hurtful, but that mindset strikes me as a little bit of mentally ill and a whole lot of miserable!

This idea of "safety" from diverse views is also misguided. I so desperately want to say to those people:

> *I have experienced being surrounded by people who hid their true thoughts and feelings from me. Trust me—you don't want to be in that hell. It truly is hell because you can't know what reality is! Counselors have terms for this horrible uncertainty: "shifting sand" and "destabilizing." You have no solid ground, no basis for operation. What thoughts or plans lurk behind that smiling face? You might never know, but if there are problems, you're better off dealing with them now!*
>
> *I'm convinced this principle applies at every level of human interaction—personal relationships, work relationships, all the way up to dialogue at the national or world level. If you insist on that safe cocoon where you only encounter people who agree with you, you'll find your world gets smaller and smaller. No two humans will align on all possible topics. To insist on that is approaching narcissism. Sooner or later, you'll realize you're living in a fantasy world filled with dishonest communication, and your inborn and just plain*

> *practical need for truth will drive you to worse anxiety, and ultimately perhaps paranoia. I certainly started to feel paranoid.*
>
> *Your "safety" becomes a hellish prison, a dangerous trap. You are far better off, far safer, to do the messy work of dealing openly with differences of opinion. And besides, THAT IS HOW GOOD SOLUTIONS ARE DEVELOPED at every level of human interaction. The best solutions come from considering all perspectives on the nature of the problem, what has already been tried, HOW it has been tried, and so on.*

Yep, that's what I would say to them. And I suppose you realize, as I do, that we all need a few skills to help that open communication produce good results. I imagine we've all seen a BAD result! Is there anyone on the face of the earth who hasn't seen a difficult conversation crash and burn?

Have you ever tried to have a friendly discussion about a polarizing topic? Have you seen this hypersensitivity and close-mindedness I'm describing? Have you even seen relationships destroyed because someone couldn't tolerate a different opinion?

That blows my mind. Let's think about this: Assuming both parties are reasonably well behaved, in what universe would that conversation cause the personal relationship to be destroyed? Maybe this is the answer—in a universe of people who have tied their self-worth to always being right.

But let that sink in for a moment. In any universe, is that a reasonable expectation? I have thought about this a lot because I've seen the problem play out so much in my life. I've decided that rejecting others purely because they think differently requires two basic assumptions:

1. I am infallible. My opinions are always right. (I won't say it this way, but that makes me God.)
2. I am so controlling, I won't even give you the freedom to be "wrong."

Wow. I find that pretty scary. What do you think? Isn't that narcissistic? As a former clinical counselor, I don't like to overuse that term, but I think in this case it fits. I've got a little theory that I've developed over the last several decades of careful observation, and it goes like this: *All children—without knowing it—follow one of two paths as they're moving through childhood and emerging into adulthood. They can unconsciously become just like one of their parents—the controlling know-it-all in this case—or they can consciously choose to be different.*

Why do some children turn out one way and some the other? I've heard this question posed as people are interviewed about their horrific childhoods: *How did they avoid becoming just like their abusive parent?*

Based on the examples I've observed, I've started to wonder if there could be some kind of spiritual connection that brings insight. This may seem strange, but I'm starting to think spiritual connection and emotional intelligence go hand in hand. Somehow, some children are able to say, "I can clearly see my parents' character flaws, and I won't repeat those mistakes, and I won't overcorrect and swing to the opposite extreme." Meanwhile, other children grow up to be EXACTLY like a hurtful parent in some way. I don't know all the factors. But in THIS case, with THIS particular trait we're discussing right now, maybe it all starts with being a lover of truth. And in my world, "truth" is synonymous with God.

But why are so many of us allowing others to act that way? That domineering behavior and hostility toward different opinions? As I've said, I think this problem is at epidemic proportions—and severe enough to lead to REJECTION over a different opinion. Yet our passivity is also an epidemic! Why are we enabling this?

Well, maybe I've just answered my own question: If we'll face rejection, and right now we can't handle that rejection, passivity is an obvious first choice. There are other options as we'll see, but passivity seems to be the default. Other options require more personal development. It seems we all fall into the easiest path, and I have been extremely passive in the past also. It's a constant struggle, isn't it?

# 8
# Breaking Old Chains

Like many others, I started my journey far, far into the passive zone. But somehow I knew I would need to ditch the passivity and learn assertiveness. I couldn't bear to remain passive and plunge into depression as a person who is never really seen or heard. But I also did not want to repeat my father's angry aggression. Getting that pendulum into the assertive middle zone—WITH RELAXED CONFIDENCE—became my long-term goal.

My first attempts sounded like aggression because I feared a backlash—with good reason. I was mentally prepared for a fight. My stress hormones were in the stratosphere, so my fear sounded like aggression, like a dog that's been abused: Underneath that nasty growl is fear.

Later on, after I had made some progress, my personal growth became more challenging, as I found myself in a group of people who were what we counselors call "avoidant." It seems they did not know how to be assertive and thought assertiveness was a horrible sin. So behind-the-back manipulation and battles for control were the norm, and individuality was despised.

For example, I once made a casual comment that I never liked dishwashers because I had to put a clean dish in to get a clean dish out. (I suspect that was true of older models in apartments where property wasn't well maintained.) Oh, my! You would have thought I had just said something terrible, because they LIKED dishwashers! I could tell they were upset and personally offended, and I secretly thought to myself, "Whoa. This is not good."

But actually, looking back, I realize it was more often the case that these people successfully HID their feelings behind a polite mask, because they believed authenticity was a path to disaster (especially when one carries a lot of shame over feelings and has never learned that communication brings greater closeness when done right). So their main obsession was dishonest avoidance.

Avoidance was king! It was like a religion! These individuals seemed to think the most honorable way of handling human interaction was to smile and act like everything's fine, but take offense, be secretive, complain behind your back, and let you know you were a horrible monster if you dared to speak up for yourself. The truth is, these people desperately needed someone to align against and blame, and I was one of several victims.

Eventually, the bullying began, and gradually, more people joined in. Wanting to keep the peace, I received the comments in silence and did my best to overlook each offense. PASSIVE!

And right here I'll share one of the reasons I WAS so passive. Some "Christians" preach conflict avoidance at all costs. They cherry-pick Bible verses to support their advice. They focus only on the phrases "live at peace with everyone," "don't judge," "turn the other cheek," and "forgive." But they fail to properly define those terms, and they ignore verses with different options for handling conflict.

The fact is, Jesus wasn't into conflict avoidance to that degree. His behavior and his instructions are proof of that. But because of childhood pain or other factors, we humans tend to overreact and let the pendulum swing too far to the side that feels EASIER or SAFER. A healthy middle is lost. Conflict avoidance at all costs leads to all kinds of evil, and that philosophy is rooted in fear, cowardice, and ignorance. Some might pat themselves on the back for being so spiritual as they misrepresent the real Jesus. So to those people, I just want to lovingly say, "Please look at what Jesus actually did, and what he instructed you to do."

This last thought sums up what I believe to be an accidental perversion of scripture that sometimes occurs in the general church community. And it can literally ruin people's lives! But my thoughts are not just relevant for people who profess to be Christian. We ALL need to be aware of ANY cultural influence—coming from ANY part of society—that is harmful to us. We're all in this together!

There truly are different possibilities for handling bullying or abuse. Amazing unconditional love in the face of bullying can sometimes work wonders. Other times, a more aggressive response might be needed, as some people have learned dealing with a grade-school bully. But silent passivity in the face of abuse only emboldens the abusers, as I learned the hard way. If your goal is to advance a cause as a martyr, you might WANT to embolden the abuser with silent passivity, as Jesus demonstrated when he chose to stand silent at certain moments. For MANY reasons, standing silent can have a special power. The question to ask yourself is, *What am I called to do in this exact moment?*

Later, when the abuse got so bad that I HAD to speak up, I was told things shouldn't bother me. That's psychological abuse.

I was told I'm "oversensitive." That's also psychological abuse. And usually hypocritical. The truth was, in this case, they were more sensitive than I was!

I was told, "That's crazy," "That never happened," or "I don't remember that." That's gaslighting.

Some individuals pretended to be on my side, but betrayed me with the others behind my back. Of course it took a while to figure this out. It was a SLOW process of gathering clues. I know of two reasons:

1. Some people have finely honed skills of deception.
2. My wishful thinking played to their advantage. I wanted to believe I had allies, and I received their assurances that I did.

The day came when I realized I had been set up and betrayed in a major way. I will never forget that moment. I couldn't have been more shocked if this individual had pulled out a knife and stabbed me in the gut. That's what it felt like. I pulled away from the worst offenders, but the behind-the-back discussions only increased.

My patience gradually dwindled to zero, and my passivity or attempts at careful assertiveness gave way to arguments and anger. Then, because I was angry, I started to worry that I was the abuser! My counselor at that time set me straight: "Carol, you're not abusive. You're REACTING TO ABUSE!"

That shows how good bullies and abusers are at twisting things and claiming everything is your fault. Even I had begun to fear they were right!

So what I want to know is, how many people have been labeled as "the problem" in a group, when they're not the problem any more than everyone else? In a troubled system, EVERYONE, sooner or later, is making a negative contribution, even if that contribution is silence, enabling, and betrayal.

At that time in my life, generally speaking, the church itself was of little help to me. Most churches didn't offer counseling. The ones that DID offer counseling seemed to have no awareness of abusive dynamics. Or in one case, the pastor became part of my trauma, making certain statements to me in private, but later, to avoid the displeasure of other church members, throwing me under the bus, claiming he had never made those statements! It was cowardice, fear of standing for his principles. Do you know a few cowards like that? I have just three comments about that betrayal:

1. Just because people are in a church or even leading a church, you can't assume they're Christian. My father was president of the Church Council when I was a kid. I later learned he was an atheist. Francis Chan, a well-known pastor and author, has said he believes 90% of the people in American churches are not really Christian. I don't know about any number, but from what I know, I have no reason to challenge his estimate.
2. I will simply say the scriptures do talk about a judgment day. If you're curious, you might want to study that.
3. I'm no longer willing to let pathetic individuals raise my stress hormones. I will forgive with the CORRECT understanding of forgiveness. I will pray for them. And I am free of them! So that's all I have to say about that! (But more on forgiveness later.)

Eventually, I developed a backbone and invited a few of these individuals to join me in attending qualified counseling or consulting. What a colossal waste of time, energy, emotional stress, and money! Professionals can't "fix" those who don't want to be fixed! As one of the counselors told me, "You have too much faith in counseling." Agreed! By then I had a master's in counseling, and more importantly, I had spent time in counseling myself, and it had been tremendously helpful—such a great opportunity to take a hard look at myself, learn and grow. That's priceless because, as the saying goes, "The unexamined life is not worth living."

So with that positive growth in my background, I couldn't understand why these people wouldn't likewise embrace an opportunity to change for the better! Why couldn't they learn and grow? *What's so hard?* I asked myself. It all seemed so simple to decide to "get healthy" and start living with integrity. I just didn't get it. I was naïve. Or maybe it's more accurate to say it this way: I was in a different place mentally and spiritually. They weren't there.

Counselors and business consultants and other helpers often encounter one or more individuals who refuse to take a hard look at themselves and others in the group. These individuals refuse to open up to painful truth. This is part of the core spiritual problem that forces people to turn to a professional for help. If all parties are spiritually capable of "the hard look," they probably don't need outside help. They're much more likely to work things out on their own.

Perhaps you're starting to understand why I say there's a spiritual dimension operating here—Jesus is famous for telling people to get the PLANK out of their own eye before worrying about the SPECK in another person's eye. **But how many people have the spiritually transformed vision to do that?**

When they can't see the ugly parts of themselves and all other group members, AND REALIZE GOD LOVES THEM ALL ANYWAY, they think the request to examine their flaws is more condemnation, and they resist that. Who can blame them? They've already experienced so much condemnation from others!

But using MY lingo, we can say hypocritical condemnation is from Satan, not God! In other words, hypocritical condemnation is an evil entity, while authentic Christianity provides protection from condemnation—accountability, yes, but also loving compassion and encouragement, NOT condemnation. To quote the apostle Paul: "Therefore, there is now no condemnation for those who are in Christ Jesus" (Rom 8:1 New International Version).

Once people understand God loves them EVEN WITH their ugly parts, they can escape their self-condemnation, grant mercy and grace first to themselves and then to others. But without that transformation that comes from feeling God's love, true peace and affection in the group hang out of reach.

**What do you want to call that kind of transformed vision? How do you explain it?**

Another reason I was slow to see the full scope of the betrayal is that I was a victim of my own optimism due to PROJECTION. We all tend to project our values onto others and assume they're on the same page. So don't be too hard on yourself if that happens. It's a painful—maybe even traumatic—lesson when we open our eyes and finally see ugly truth. But if it happens, I would encourage you to remember who you are, get right back up, and carry on. Rejoice! They don't win!

Perhaps this famous line from the apostle Paul will bring you comfort: "We are hard pressed on every side, but not crushed; perplexed, but not in despair; persecuted, but not abandoned; struck down, but not destroyed" (2 Cor 4:8–9 NIV). That's determination. That's persistence. That's heroism!

Eventually I started to accept the futility of my efforts. I told one of these helpers, "I'm just beating my head against the wall!"

"Yes," she said, "and we've got to get you away from the wall."

That was a turning point, but I still needed to learn how to survive this kind of warfare. I began to work single-mindedly on MY OWN BEHAVIOR. I was gradually learning to act calm no matter what. I realized I HAD to stay calm and nonchalant, because if I didn't, I only handed them ammunition—the ability to say, "See? Look at how she's behaving. I told you she was unstable."

One individual seemed to love "stirring the pot," creating conflict and drama. Here's how the game was played: *Behave in a way that pushes her buttons. And lie to her! That usually gets her going!* Of course, this was never done when others were listening. Some people are masters at posing as a good person but creating hell when no one else is looking.

During my earlier attempts to find qualified help or emotional support, I found that those rare church counselors sometimes were too naïve to see through the false front. I don't know, but I gradually developed a theory that they had lived such a sheltered life, they weren't up to the job of fighting evil. Or maybe it's more accurate to say they weren't spiritually attuned. **But I think fighting evil is part of a church's job description. Shouldn't it be?**

It takes a very savvy or "spirit-filled" helper to see what's really going on. I recall one article that warned all helpers of the possibility of deception. It said something like this: If you're not careful, you'll think the victim is the abuser and the abuser is the victim. That's because the abuser is a master manipulator and sits there calmly, appearing to have nothing but the best of intentions. The victim, meanwhile, is unkempt, irritable, argumentative, and practically hysterical.

When I discovered that article, I said to myself, "Man! That's me!" At times, I was that irritable and argumentative person! I was frustrated when the one posing as a helper wouldn't confront the lies and empty excuses when they were exposed. And I had grown tired of a counseling world where you get 50 minutes per week, and at the end of the session, you hear, "Oops! We're out of time. Have a good week." *HAVE A GOOD WEEK?*

**We Americans should be living in a nation of caring citizens who have been taught to listen and nurture one another, with little need for paid counselors. Instead, in the counseling field, we have this impersonal and artificial system run by insurance companies. I've WORKED in that system—I could give many reasons why it needs a complete overhaul.**

But here's one thing I learned from those sessions with counselors, consultants, and other types of helpers: With regard to the narcissistic abuser who masquerades as a good and caring person, when the helper looks at the history and calls the abuser's bluff, the abuser's true colors will finally be revealed.

Fooling people is a satisfying exercise in power and control for the abuser. Such people have grown ACCUSTOMED to fooling people. This is one way they comfort themselves that they are superior. Secretly on the inside, they are laughing at how they have duped others, and they think of more trusting individuals as stupid and gullible. So when this source of "supply" for ego gratification momentarily disappears, and they realize somebody sees past their façade, they're capable of completely freaking out.

How do I know? Because in this case, the freaking out consisted of going ballistic in the session and yelling three or four inches from the side of my head! I don't recall what the yelling was about. I just knew I was witnessing what happens when an abuser realizes the power to deceive has at least momentarily slipped away, and a bit of being held accountable has arrived.

So here's a solemn warning to anyone who functions as a counselor, consultant, coach, mentor, supervisor, manager, spiritual guide, healing practitioner, deliverance minister, or really anyone in any helping capacity, regardless of whether you're paid or volunteer, and regardless of your credentials or job title: **You had better know what you're doing.** You need courage and strength and spiritual discernment so that you can see evil, and you MUST cultivate that humility I mentioned—eager to learn and willing to examine your mistakes:

> *Did I jump to conclusions about what this person was about to say and interrupt based on that wrong conclusion? Did I ask this person to summarize the history but then immediately lecture the individual about a need to look forward, not backward? Did I react out of my own emotional issues and discredit or blame the victim?*

You don't all have to handle abusive situations, but you need to be able to recognize abuse so that you can refer out to someone who CAN help. And if you don't have a list of good referrals ready to go, you are violating a moral code, and perhaps your professional code of ethics.

Anyway, once I found a competent helper for myself (and I would add, once I had grown spiritually enough that I was READY to learn: "When the student is ready, the teacher will appear." –Lao Tzu), I learned to stay calm and cheerful no matter what. As a lover of truth, I realized one of my vulnerable areas was hearing a lie. I would find myself getting sucked into an argument and becoming frustrated. But now I would say, "Well, I don't buy that," and walk away. Of course, that individual followed me and tried to continue the conversation. It was too much fun, this game of cat and mouse.

Yes, over a span of time in this group, what I had originally seen as betrayal due to fear and cowardice, I now realized was purposeful cruelty. It became clear that I was caught in an evil game of cat and mouse, which included passive aggression, deception, lying, betrayal, pitting people against one another, and an apparent delight when inflicting pain. I hadn't considered the possibility that some of these people ENJOYED seeing that look of shock and pain on my face. I would go into a session and say, "I don't get it. How can people be that stupid? I've explained six times this hurts my feelings."

But it was time to wake up and smell the coffee, you might say. I have no doubt my ability to discern and accept the truth developed in me because I had been growing spiritually by the grace of God. This was a two-part improvement.

The first part was SEEING someone's true character. That's the discernment part. Generally, the more spiritually developed we are, the faster we can see right through someone. Childhood wounding can slow that spiritual development and clear vision. But that ability to discern can become simply amazing. There have been times when I had discernment we could call "supernatural." I could predict someone's behavior or correctly discern the person's character. One time, it happened in the first second of meeting that person! It was an eerie experience, but beneficial.

The second part was ACCEPTING the ugly truth, which comes from knowing I will be okay no matter what, knowing I am a child of God, I don't NEED their approval, something better is ahead, I am NOT what those abusers said about me, I am NOT to blame for their cruel behavior, and I do NOT deserve that kind of treatment. **It doesn't matter WHAT I could have possibly done. No one deserves abuse!**

That last part seems obvious to you, I hope. But I had been so wounded that, deep down, I had doubts about all that. And abusers work hard to explain to you what YOU did to CAUSE their abusive behavior—not that they'll admit they're abusive. But somehow you earned their contempt, and they think they're justified. That, of course, is a lie from the pit of hell.

In more recent years, when I felt I needed to tell someone a bit of that story, I would hear, "You don't seem like the kind of person that would have put up with that!"

"Well, I've changed," I would say. Yes, I grew spiritually, and I am incredibly relieved.

But do you see how these two parts are linked? The ability to SEE ugly truth depends upon a deep sense of identity and wellbeing that tells you, *No matter what, even if I lose my career or finances or reputation or friends or family, I'm still okay, and probably far better off in the long run. It will be one heroic, adventurous, joy-filled journey. Everything's going to be okay.*

People usually don't comprehend this change in identity until they experience it. It's hard to describe in words. When you get this new identity through your head, you see life in a whole new way. I don't want you to think any of us can reach a place where life is 100% bliss. We'll always need to battle fear and other universal human weaknesses. We'll always be monitoring our unhelpful thoughts and "taking every thought captive."

**That's where scripture comes in, from what I've experienced. It shows you the way out of your mental prison. And we're not just talking about serious issues like abuse. There isn't a human on the face of the earth who doesn't feel some kind of pain or have something that needs improvement. And change is hard. And we're often our own worst enemy.**

So scripture can be helpful, especially because it's REALISTIC. For example, Jesus said, "…In this world you will have trouble. But take heart! I have overcome the world" (John 16:33 NIV).

This change of identity is the core of authentic Christianity. People who have not experienced that kind of healing may think of

Christianity and other religions as just following a bunch of rules and thinking you're better than everyone else.

Jesus HATED that!

But isn't that one of the ways people view "religion" in general? Following a set of rules or practices and thinking of oneself as somehow superior for having the "right" answers? But from what I know, authentic Christianity is NOT that. Authentic Christianity teaches AGAINST that. That doesn't mean there aren't some right answers for a happy life. It means there's no room for an attitude of superiority: "for all have sinned and fall short of the glory of God" (Rom 3:23 NIV).

Remember when I mentioned Francis Chan and the 90% that supposedly aren't Christian? Again I'll say I have no idea about any number, but maybe they're the ones who have given so many people that bad impression. All I can say is, they sure aren't doing what Jesus told them to do.

If you don't obey your leader's instructions, how can you claim to be a follower?

# 9

# Deeper into My Past

At this point I imagine some of you are feeling confused: *I don't get it. Why was she slow to take action? MY dad was horrible—way worse than that—and I didn't fall into self-doubt or abuse!*

I can understand having that question. I don't know that I can fully answer such a deep question. The first thing we need to understand is that none of us should try to earn some kind of competitive award for having a worse life.

I became more aware of this a few years ago when I was staying briefly with a friend who had been through horrible childhood sexual abuse. One day, I went to lunch with a different friend, and I learned she had also been through shocking childhood trauma. I was gone a long time because I believe in being a good listener and taking time to be fully present when people gather the courage to share their heart.

When I returned to the first friend's house, I mentioned that my lunch conversation was long because I was learning about this friend's horrible childhood. The two women did not know each other, or even each other's names, and I didn't supply more detail—I was just explaining why I was gone so long.

To my surprise, this friend came toward me with an angry retort that started with, "Oh? Well, was it as bad as…?" She finished that sentence by supplying a disgusting description of sexual abuse.

I knew this friend had some emotional issues, but I sure wasn't expecting that outburst! The only thing I could think to say was, "It's not a competition."

Fortunately, she realized she was out of line and apologized. I felt sorry for her because I knew she had to be carrying tremendous anger after all those years. Anyway, it just doesn't work to compare people. Each of us is different. And the motivation to make that comparison doesn't seem healthy.

The second idea I want to share is a meme that shows a horizontal line labeled, "Someone's life." At the far right end of the line is a tiny, bracketed portion labeled, "What you know about it." The heading of the meme is, "Why You Should Be Gentle With People."

So if you're already having questions, doubts, or—heaven forbid—negative judgments, thank you for demonstrating what we're all up against. One of our biggest enemies (and a big blessing) is our brains' tendency to try to make rapid sense of things and form judgments. It's a survival mechanism—we fear danger. The faster we form judgments, the better we feel. Because we tend to rush to judgment, I favor pursuing the opposite. I see value in uncertainty and self-doubt in the short term. I see that as the doorway to Wisdom. And I want to keep that door open as long as possible. That means I've learned to value patience while waiting for things to become clear. Sometimes we even have to accept that things will never become clear in this lifetime.

But while I've spoken against that human rush to judgment, I also wrote about a spiritual discernment that developed within me. In those cases, I knew something instantly in a supernatural way. The difference between the two situations is found in this question: *At what point do we pronounce our judgments to be right?*

Those who "rush to judgment" pronounce their judgments to be right instantly. In my examples of spiritual discernment, I could only pronounce them to be right once I saw the reality manifest and prove my spiritual discernment correct. And even then, we have to guard against creating our own self-fulfilling prophecy—we have to ensure we don't act in a way that CREATES our original prediction. I am confident I didn't do that in those cases.

Back to that horizontal line! I want to give you a few more glimpses of that line. Not because I need to defend myself against negative judgments. Not because I am looking for sympathy. Not because I have a valid need to vent and be heard—I've received enough help and healing that I'm past that need to feel understood regarding my past. I'll share more only because it's part of my sacred story, and it might help someone.

**Part of my spiritual growth has been learning to do what I feel called to do and leave the rest to God.** *Give up that human desire for approval. Give up that human craving for understanding. I'll even give up my attachment to a good result!*

**Here's my thought:** *Do what you feel called to do and don't worry about the rest! Just let it all go and be free. Ahhhh! Relief!*

So here's more of "the line."

# 10

## The Road Runner

There was a lot of death in my family when I was young. When I was a year old, a close relative died in a car accident. The next year, my mother's mother died of cancer. She had been sent home to die ELEVEN years earlier by a prestigious medical institution. That's our first example of learning we can't always trust what the medical establishment tells us.

Her death devastated my mother: Years later, she told me, "Boy, when my mother died, that really knocked me for a loop!" I also knew her thoughts and feelings from spending many, many hours listening to her talk about her past.

Looking back, I see that time in our lives more clearly now. I see a wonderful woman who had just been through too much. She had suffered through childhood with an abusive sister, alcoholic father, and a distant mother. She had cared for her ailing mom for more than eleven years. She had miscarried her second pregnancy. A close relative had died two years earlier, and her mother had died one year earlier. She was now at home with me, her third living child, a child that was not planned. (Near the end of his life my father told me they had planned to be done after two. My thought was and is, *Well, God had other plans!*)

I also later learned that we kids were not well chaperoned during those years. We had been expected to potty train ourselves, for one thing: If we had an accident, we were to clean up the mess ourselves. It seems no one was there to help. No one was there to encourage or praise. We were expected to handle that important developmental stage alone. I can also recall wandering the neighborhood alone. I don't know for sure, but I think the signs are there: My mom was probably struggling with lifelong depression.

So I think all of that set the stage for the Road Runner incident. Road Runner was our parakeet. He was called "Road Runner" because, of all the parakeets we owned over all my growing-up years, he was the only one that would not fly. He ran around on the floor and I enjoyed chasing him. Maybe you already see it coming. I wish I had. But I was just a three-year-old. As I chased Road Runner down the bedroom hallway, I decided I'd step on his tail to stop him, just as kids might grab a cat's tail. My foot came down too far forward. To my horror, I saw Road Runner was no longer moving.

In my little three-year-old mind, I must have figured out he was dead. I ran into my parents' bedroom, climbed onto the perfectly-made bed, and curled up on the pillows. I was crying hard. The last thing I remember, my mother must have come into the room because I heard her say, "Carol, what happened to the bird?"

I think I started to answer but then…That's it. My memory goes black. Boom. SHUT OFF—except that I have one very hazy memory, a memory so hazy it's like trying to see through layers of gray gauze in a shadowy room at dusk: I think I recall my mother angrily telling me to pick up the bird. I was being ordered to clean up my mess. Other than that hazy memory, nothing.

I can't know what I experienced that day. I don't know what I was thinking or feeling. But based on what I have shared so far, I assume my world went very dark that day. My #1 connection was angry with me, and there was hell to pay. I don't fully know: What do those feelings of guilt, shame, and rejection do to a three-year-old child?

In piecing the story together, I see more signs things had not gone well for me. The next thing I remember, it was evening and the entire family was in the basement. They were all standing at the laundry machines, placing the bird into a shoebox and preparing for a little funeral in the backyard. I was sitting on the basement stairs, far away from everyone else. Someone called to me, "Carol, come on over."

I remember my arms were folded across my chest and I shouted "No!" I think I was sobbing as well. I was one very angry little girl. What happened to cause that anger?

A counselor once asked me, "Did anyone come over to you? Pick you up? Comfort you?"

"No," I said.

I had not even thought of that. When you're a kid, all you know is what you know. You don't KNOW what's "normal" or "healthy." You don't know what else is possible. You don't precisely know what you're missing. And the experts say your default logic is to blame yourself—for everything. Why? The explanation I've heard is that, when you're a child and at the mercy of your parents, it would be too horrifying to fully comprehend that your parents are not behaving correctly, and you are trapped in this horrifying world.

*But if I'm to blame, then I have some power and control. Maybe I can change what I do and make the situation better.* THAT is the idea that saves us from complete insanity.

*Things aren't so hopeless, because maybe I can cause things to get better.* THAT is the hope that keeps us going.

You may be wondering, *Didn't you learn more about this day from your family as the years went by?* No. The incident was not discussed as far as I recall. Decades later, when my mother was no longer around, at the dinner table one evening, my father mentioned that he and my siblings had recently discussed that day. I acknowledged I knew what they were talking about.

My father said, "Oh. We were hoping you didn't recall that because we figured it was traumatic."

I saw my sister studying me carefully as the tears welled up in my eyes. What's even MORE traumatic, if you ask me, is that there WAS no discussion, just as there was no open discussion about other family problems. And there were no apologies from my mom during her lifetime. Likewise with my dad—no apologies for anything. Likewise among my siblings. None that I recall, anyway.

I actually don't think a single traumatic experience has nearly the same damaging power as the day-in, day-out dysfunction that can exist in a family. I think it's that drip-drip-drip of repetitive smaller mistakes—that consistent failure to do the better thing—that does the most damage. I know at least some experts agree with me.

**And that's why I appreciate authentic Christianity.** Parents who've committed their lives to being the best person they can be still make mistakes—sometimes very big ones as I have done—but they are spiritually strong enough to recognize those mistakes, grieve over them, apologize, make amends, and commit to change. **This, in my view, is the opposite of dysfunction.**

None of us is perfect. We're all just struggling down the road together. When we stay humble, accept our brokenness, feel God's love and forgiveness, and grant others grace, life can be a much more peaceful, more healing, healthier, happier journey, and things can gradually get better and better rather than worse and worse. People can grow closer and closer rather than further and further apart.

And that's good news for all of us! Each little thing you do right is so important. DOING THE NEXT RIGHT THING, step by step. That's where victory is accomplished! Think of the Olympic athletes—they'll tell you. Victory is secured in the day-in, day-out consistency, through good days and bad. And if you have one bad day, if you have a failure, you get right back up and keep going. You grant yourself grace, and you keep going.

That's where true heroism lives! I think our culture is far too obsessed with the single glorious winning moment, or the single traumatic moment—maybe because it makes a more dramatic story. But life is won or lost where there are no cheering crowds, and it's just you alone, you and God, in all those moments when you don't FEEL LIKE doing what you need to do, but you make yourself do it anyway. And when you "fall off the wagon," you just get right back on and keep going. It's okay.

Right now, you are bound to be battling something because that's how life is. Even though I'm struggling too, I want you to understand something revolutionary and liberating: **We are actually wired for struggle. Truly living means taking on a challenge.** Don't believe the lie that life should be easy. Have you seen this quotation?

> "To avoid criticism, do nothing, say nothing, and be nothing."
> –Adapted from Elbert Hubbard

**You can become one of the great heroes of the world just by doing the right thing in the next moment, and then building your success one step at a time.**

Steel yourself, because you might face opposition. Or maybe your biggest battle will be with yourself. For this effort, some divine assistance helps. I know in MY life, when I tried to handle things on my own, I rushed into blunders that made things worse. That hurt ME most of all. If I had slowed down, gotten quiet, and listened for that "still, small voice," I would have enjoyed a much better life.

# 11

## Enticement, Deception, Betrayal

I don't feel called to tell this next story in vivid detail, but it may help someone to know I also experienced sexual abuse as a child. My parents were not involved and never knew about it, as far as I know.

As you probably know, childhood sexual abuse is a common problem. In my case, the predator was a step-grandfather. If you've studied the subject, you know that the abuse usually starts with "grooming behavior." This might include giving the child extra attention, getting closer, and gradually testing boundaries. Children are naturally sexually curious beginning around age three and increasing gradually, so almost any child could be vulnerable to such advances. When I was six, the next phase involved being deceived, led into a trap, and molested. The shock and betrayal of trust were two more examples of trauma that occurred in my life, and again, as a child, I did not have a way to see all of that as an adult would.

Decades later, I was surprised at my own reaction when finally "confessing" this experience to a counselor. I broke down crying and apologizing as though I was confessing a horrible crime. Well, it WAS something I take a certain amount of personal responsibility for, despite my young age. I knew I was doing something wrong, but the curiosity and temptation were there. That's how sin works sometimes. The trap looks enticing. Curiosity might get the better of us. The early bits of attention feel good. We think somehow this will end well. But with sin, the end is always bad news, one way or another.

I think it's psychologically and spiritually healthy for me to take responsibility for the part I played. I knew I was doing something wrong, and I of course have repented of that. So with that said, we can now turn to what today's experts might prefer that I say: *I was a child. I'm not to blame for the actions of the abuser. The shame does not belong to me.*

I get it. I agree with that about 99.33% of the way. I agree 100% with the first sentence, 100% with the second sentence, and 98% with the third sentence! I understand the damage they're trying to undo. That's why I broke down the way I did when I finally told my story to the counselor. I was carrying a huge trunk of shame that was not mine to carry. That load of toxic shame is what the experts are trying to relieve me of when they start with, "You were just a child."

When I was done with my story, my counselor did a beautiful thing to help eliminate the shame. He simply said, "Thank you for sharing your sacred story with me."

I must have looked at him like he had three heads. *SACRED STORY?* But this technique is what we counselors call a "reframe," and it really helped me. It's also TRUE. By recasting my experience as something sacred, and of course by avoiding judgment or shaming, he started me on my healing journey.

I do appreciate the lifting of shame that experts offer. But in my spirit, I will never believe it's right for me to claim to be 100% victim. As I said, I knew I was doing something wrong, and while I won't take the blame for HIS behavior, and I won't carry HIS shame, I have owned my personal responsibility, and I'm convinced that's a healthy thing to do. So in my heart, I finished the process of:
- acknowledging my guilt
- recognizing which shame did NOT belong to me
- recognizing the smaller amount of shame that DID belong to me
- receiving God's forgiveness for the part that was mine.

It's a process that feels like getting a tremendous weight off my chest, off my back, and out of my mind. Relief! What do you think? Do you see how useful it can be to take responsibility for the part you played in any kind of problem? I think it's incredibly healthy. Those are the people I want to be around—they own their own faults and mistakes. I respect them and I'm doing my best to be one of them. Then I get to respect ME.

We're talking about walking in TRUTH, the WHOLE truth. And the truth really does set you free, even if it's painful. When you own what's yours to own, you can breathe free. You can be yourself, finally. You no longer need to fear criticism. You gladly receive what's true and helpful and you discard the rest. As the saying goes, "When someone dumps a garbage can of criticism on you, look for the treasure in the trash." No matter how nasty that other person is, there just might be a piece of treasure in the trash. Look for it and gain even more peace of mind. Own what's yours, fix any problem that might exist, discard the rest, and go in peace.

I don't believe you can have peace of mind if you rush to discard all of it instantly. The truth will haunt you and eat at your soul and change what you see in the mirror, whether you realize it or not. And if there's nothing in there that SHOULD haunt you, you gain even more peace and strength by moving honestly through the examination process.

**Your own gut-wrenching honesty is your path to strength and peace of mind. So maybe it comes down to one question: DO YOU HAVE THE COURAGE TO FACE THE TRUTH?**

I mean REALLY face the truth. Can you FEEL, for example, how you made another person feel? Can you SEE how another individual could have a different perspective with a different but equally valid set of priorities? **You've been called to greatness— I'm sure of that. And this is your necessary first step.**

This is not just the wisdom of secular counseling. This is also the genius of authentic Christianity. Christians call it "repentance." The word's origin literally means turning in the opposite direction, doing an about-face, and changing patterns of thinking. When you do that about-face, you face up to—YOU CONFRONT—all your fears and failures and bad memories and your dark side and everything else that's making you miserable. We can call all of that "the monster."

**We turn and face the monster, and our courageous journey begins. Then we begin to heal and thrive. It is a heroic journey.**

Well, I could end on that happy note, but there's an extra twist to this story you should know. That step-grandfather was married to my father's mother. As you'll recall, my other grandmother died when I was two. This remaining grandmother was very special to me. She did all the grandmotherly things that grandmothers do. I have cherished memories of things as simple as sitting on her lap while she read the newspaper comics to me. I felt unconditional love from her—I could share certain thoughts or feelings, knowing I wouldn't be judged or criticized.

She paid for my sewing lessons and gave me additional instruction at her home. We made stuffed animals and Barbie clothes. I loved being with her. Of course, that meant being in the same house as the abuser. I never told her about the abuse. I had fought him off and kept my distance after that first attack, if I remember correctly. But I still had to put up with his presence, his weird remarks, and his own version of cat and mouse: If I happened to be passing through a hallway and my grandmother was elsewhere, he would act like he was going to grab me again. Terrorized, I would skitter away from him and go on my way.

The threat of encountering him was especially scary if my grandmother needed a piece of sewing fabric. They kept the fabric in boxes in the old coal room, behind the octopus-like furnace in the basement. If she sent me down to retrieve a piece of fabric, *Oh no! Maybe he's down there waiting for me! Or maybe he'll appear before I make my way back upstairs!*

Looking back, I realize that was a terrifying way to live. Probably as a result, I was plagued with a strange "nausea," a systemic sick feeling, which might go away after eating. I now assume that was emotional stress. But it all seemed normal to me. I maybe recall one episode where he did confront me in that coal room. That memory is extra, extra hazy. I hope I was able to escape without much contact, assuming it did happen and was not something I dreamed.

My grandmother died when I was 14, and after that, all contact with the abuser was done. A few years later, he died alone in that house. Apparently, he had contracted some form of leukemia. The neighbors eventually realized they had not seen him coming or going. I assume they called the police. He was found on the floor in his bedroom, dead for several days. I later helped my mom clean the house and prepare it for sale. The smell of death was still there. His body fluids had soaked into the hardwood floor.

According to my mother, it was at this point that the neighbors told her what had been happening. It seems the abuser enjoyed other kinds of abuse. They were aware he would beat my grandmother. I assume they could hear things going on in the house.

And they did nothing.

Why didn't they say something to my parents? My mother said they would've gladly had my grandmother live with us if they had known. I would've loved that, and I might've been spared more trauma. Why didn't they call the police?

Well, I know that times were different back then. Women were in a more subservient role, and our culture was less able to handle abuse and other social problems.

**So here's the significant moment I want to share with you:** More than three decades after their deaths, I was doing nothing in particular around my house, not even thinking about my past, when suddenly this question popped into my mind: *Who keeps sewing fabric in a filthy dirty coal room?*

I recalled being taken down there by BOTH my grandmother and step-grandfather and being shown the boxes of sewing fabric in the coal room.

In an instant, I knew: My grandmother had been part of the setup.

In the next instant I thought, *But I forgive you.*

As you know, I had learned long ago that she was an abused woman. I have never counseled others in the abuse field, but I knew what could happen to the minds of abused women. And, as others have suggested, he may have threatened to do even worse things if she didn't play along.

Why was I so quick to forgive? Maybe we could say I saw her as God would see her—pathetic and weak and lost. Doesn't absolve her of responsibility, but I could understand better in that moment who she really was. What a sad life. I felt sorry for her. And I still loved her. Despite that truth, I will always love her, just as I love and forgive all those who have hurt me in some way.

But the irony of it all wasn't lost on me: THE ONE PERSON IN MY LIFE WHO I THOUGHT WAS MY ONLY SOURCE OF UNCONDITIONAL LOVE had betrayed me to an abuser. A few years later, I finished my healing in that area by visiting their graves. Had a little monologue for each of them. Let them both know I forgive them. But I didn't mince words with either of them.

Some of you may be wondering how I could possibly say I forgive them both. It's a natural human thing to crave justice. Maybe you've had experiences that gave you that craving. Believe me, I understand a craving for justice. In my view, that craving is not at all a human weakness or an ugly human trait. It's part of our divine identity. God is not just a God of love and mercy. He's also a God of justice. So I believe it's a natural, inborn tendency we all have, deep in our gut, to crave justice, to want to see justice done. I think we're hardwired that way.

But we humans tend to be pro-justice for others, but pro-mercy for ourselves. We lean toward hypocrisy. That's certainly not right! Therefore, scripture makes it clear that we will not be forgiven if we don't forgive others, and in the Bible God says, "Vengeance is mine; I will repay…" (Deut 32:35 Berean Standard Bible).

Is that just another Bible verse that serves as "opium for the masses"? Is it just a man-made promise designed to stop people from killing each other? Well, we could do a whole book on that question, but the idea I want to explore is that Biblical instruction is there to keep us from destroying ourselves.

I've written a little booklet about the correct understanding of forgiveness, as part of my Myth Buster series. Every title in the series is the myth I'm about to refute, and that booklet is titled *Forgiveness Means Being a Doormat*. I'll refer you there for a longer discussion, but here I'll just say forgiveness has nothing to do with enabling the wrongdoer, agreeing to be mistreated, or condoning the behavior. It doesn't mean we can't impose consequences. We don't even have to remain in contact if distance is warranted. And forgiveness does not require that we forget.

Instead, forgiveness means we're claiming the final victory. Those people will have no power over us anymore. We might have some permanent damage, but we'll cut that damage down to the absolute minimum, and then God will take that remaining damage and create something beautiful. We won't raise our stress hormones over those people anymore. They don't deserve that kind of power. So we let go of our bitterness and desire for revenge. We just let it all go and leave the problem to God. That way, we can relieve our suffering to the greatest extent possible. With forgiveness, we help ourselves most of all.

I love the saying, "Failing to forgive is like drinking a bottle of poison and waiting for the other person to die." When we apply forgiveness correctly, we take power away from the wrongdoer, and we get the poison out of our systems. So the verse that states, "Vengeance is mine…" which is God speaking in the Bible, is basically saying, "You are my beloved. I don't want you to suffer any more over this. I'll take that burden for you. Let me handle this."

It might help to imagine a movie. You are in the role of a sweet little child. A bad guy did you wrong. Your big strong Daddy holds you, comforts you, sings over you, and when you're ready, tells you that you can return to playing happily out in the garden. You feel the warm sunshine on your shoulders, smell the different flowers and feel their glossy leaves or fuzzy leaves. You hear the birds singing, admire the beautiful blue sky and fluffy white clouds, poke at a bug with a stick. Meanwhile, big strong Daddy will fix the situation for you.

You don't hope He goes and kills the guy. That would be taking back some of that poisonous hatred. You just don't let the wrongdoer have space in your head, except for one brilliant move—you are now so strong and so filled with love that you can pray that the wrongdoer repents and finds God. That's peace. That's victory. That's a partial return to your innocence. That's freedom, and one example of "turning the world upside down."

Once, after talking at length with a prominent religious leader about what I'd been through, his closing comment to me at the end of our meeting was, "Go play." I understood what he meant. So I hope to pass this wisdom on to you.

Sometimes I wonder if people can be divided into two categories—the truly evil and unrepentant, and the rest of us who are bumbling along, trying to do the best we can. I believe the truly evil and unrepentant have an open invitation to face their ugliness and join the rest of us in a state of forgiveness. I know that many of them refuse that invitation. But for those who accept that invitation, there is a peace.

One of the best illustrations of that peace comes in the closing scene of the 1984 movie *Places in the Heart*. I would love for you to watch that movie carefully, study the faces of all the characters, and see whom you recognize in the closing scene. I must let the scene speak for itself, so that's all I will say.

# 12

## Treasuring Life

I've heard experts say people who go through what I've been through don't make it. They wind up mentally ill, in prison, or suicidal. I would add, "And the evidence suggests they're more likely to experience cancer."

In addition to my faith, I think I've been protected and pulled back from the edge by a profound esteem for life itself. Those are two sets of values that have always pulled me though. I've often thought the death in my family and the stories my mother told for years afterward gave me a profound understanding of how fragile life is and how it can't be taken for granted. I also found tremendous inspiration in a scene from the play *Our Town* by Thornton Wilder.

This play is so full of great moments and inspiring thoughts—it's no wonder it won the Pulitzer Prize! I highly recommend you give it a read, because it offers much more wisdom than I'm about to share. When I was 14 and my grandmother died with no warning,

I was about to perform a scene from that play in my high school drama class.

For those who aren't familiar, *Our Town* is about ordinary life in Grover's Corners, New Hampshire, in the late 1800s and early 1900s. The play is unusual in that there's very little set. A single table and chairs might represent a kitchen. A teenager looking out his second-floor bedroom window onto a moonlit night is really just standing on a stepladder. When we visit the cemetery in Act Three, we see only rows of wooden chairs with people—the dead—sitting there. Another unusual feature is the "Stage Manager," who comes out and speaks directly to the audience as well as to the characters.

In Act Three, Emily has died in childbirth and joins the dead in the cemetery. As the dead talk among themselves, Emily realizes she can go back and relive a day of her life. Her dead mother-in-law warns her not to do it, but Emily turns to the Stage Manager for confirmation. He acknowledges that she can indeed return, but it will be painful, because she'll see what the living could not see and she'll know the future.

Emily persists and chooses her twelfth birthday. It's breakfast time and the start of another school day. Emily participates in the conversation for a while, but then breaks down crying and begging her mother to look at her. She complains to the Stage Manager, "It goes so fast. We don't have time to look at one another."

Her mother, however, can only hear what Emily said in life. She remains unaware of this supernatural visitation. Finally, Emily tells the Stage Manager she's ready to return to her grave. But first, she delivers a monologue, saying goodbye to all the simple pleasures of life—things like clocks ticking, food and coffee, new-ironed dresses and hot baths, sleeping and waking up. She ends with this: "Oh, Earth! You're too wonderful for anyone to realize you."

She then asks the Stage Manager, "Do any human beings realize life while they live it? Every, every minute?"

The Stage Manager shakes his head: "No. Saints and poets, maybe. They do some."

Because my beloved grandmother had just died, I don't know how I made it through performing that scene. But the play has always had a special place in my heart, and its message speaks to my soul. Ever since, I've made it my goal to stay focused on how precious every moment is, even in the worst of times. I think it's a perspective worth cultivating, even though we won't always be successful.

Here again, we can see the truth that adversity brings some of our greatest gifts. I didn't want to lose my grandmother. The following year, I lost my grandfather on my mother's side. He was the last of my biological grandparents. I remember feeling sorry for myself, telling my mother it wasn't fair—other kids I knew still had their grandparents. *WHY ME?* But I was learning a hard lesson that later sustained me through hellish times. There's a beauty to life no matter what. Survivors of concentration camps have testified to this power of the human spirit. Every moment is a wonderful opportunity: Can we make the most of life?

I have tried to spread this message to others. But most people can't see it. I understand the futility expressed by the dead in the play. As Emily and the other dead people say, most living people just don't understand. Or maybe they DO recognize the fragility and brevity of life, but they react by becoming even more self-centered. The heartbreaking thing is that many of life's opportunities need the cooperation of others. If they're blind to all this, or devoted to self-gratification, there's not much we can do other than pray. What a tragedy! What a cascade of lost opportunities!

In the play, the now-deceased alcoholic church organist, Simon Stimson, says to Emily after she has returned to her grave, "Yes, now you know…That's what it was to be alive. To move about in a cloud of ignorance; to go up and down trampling on the feelings of those…of those about you…To be always at the mercy of one self-centered passion, or another…."

Emily's mother-in-law provides some balance when she says, "Now, Simon, that ain't the whole truth and you know it."

So yes, the problem is there. But life is not all doom and gloom. We can make a difference. And we can find others who are making a difference and band together to encourage one another, because it's tough out there!

One thing we can take care of is our own mindset. I've read one technique is to imagine, whatever we're doing, this will be the last time we do it: *This is the last time I will ever iron a piece of clothing. I'll apply the hot steam iron, feel the warmth and that little cloud of moisture, smell that unique aroma as the wrinkles disappear before my eyes, hear the hiss as I set the iron upright again.*

The shirt-ironing example is not exciting, but maybe that's why the writer used it. The most ordinary task can be transformed into something pleasurable or memorable. Then with our human interactions, we awaken to new possibilities: *As I approach this person, I'll remember there will come a day when I'm on my deathbed, looking back at my life and surveying every moment. I realize I'll see lost opportunity and wish I had treated this moment differently, not just in my closest relationships, but even with a coworker, a store clerk, or someone in the elevator with me. I have a choice. I can make this moment ordinary and boring and focus on my worries, or I can look other people in the eye and make their life better somehow. I can be fully present in the moment I've been given. I can brighten their day, and brighten mine as well.*

**It's not just religion that teaches people to do something nice for others. Science has now shown we physically benefit from bringing joy to others.**

That's the interesting thing about doing good in general. For thousands of years religious leaders and wise philosophers have advocated doing good. Most of the time, humans have thought of those behaviors as self-sacrificial—just giving, giving, giving. And human nature tends to be selfish, so we often resist the advice. Well now, science is proving that what has been advocated for thousands of years turns out to be beneficial even from a SELFISH perspective: Body chemistry changes. Serotonin, dopamine, and oxytocin rise. The stress hormone, cortisol, drops. Pulse rate and blood pressure drop. Physical health improves. Depression leaves. Relationships improve. Lifespan lengthens. Happiness returns!

**As a human race, we have come to a place where scientific knowledge now tells us that being self-focused is SELF-DESTRUCTIVE. Those who continue to violate this ancient advice are destroying their own happiness and slowly killing themselves!**

So all the wise philosophers and religious leaders from all the centuries of human history now have the right to say, "We told you so." But I imagine they would resist that temptation!

As a cancer patient, I have made it my job to study the cutting-edge research the last few years. I realize you probably haven't, but now you've heard this news. And you have a choice. I'm reminded of a famous passage in the Bible, Deuteronomy 30:19 English Standard Version: "…I have set before you life and death, blessing and curse. Therefore choose life, that you and your offspring may live."

We always have a choice. And as many have said, "Even NOT choosing is choosing." There is no escape. And here's a quotation I also love, which comes from the poet Robert Frost: "The only way out is through."

Take it from one who has been "through." There are great things waiting for you on the other side. Despite my introduction, that's something I can say with confidence. And here's another: **You are precious and you are worthy.**

# 13

# Obstacles to Personal Growth, Perhaps

After so many years of life experience, I think I have a fairly comprehensive view of how people can react to any exchange of ideas. Some people grab helpful information and use it to fuel their personal growth and solve problems. Other individuals are already working on some of those areas, so they feel happy to have discovered a like-minded individual, a kindred spirit.

On the other hand, here are a few reactions that are considered "negative." They tend to be obstacles to personal growth. But we all have negative reactions of one sort or another, and they can serve as smoke detectors—those unpleasant feelings warn us that a problem needs to be solved. So if we're willing to learn from them, even the so-called obstacles to personal growth can FUEL that growth!

**As with so much of what I've already shared, we have at least two ways of using this information: We can see if it applies to US, and we can prepare to encounter others with these traits.**

## *Feeling Threatened or Hostile*

We also might say "irritated," "offended," you name it. When those feelings hit, we can remind ourselves not to jump to conclusions. Slowing our reaction and asking others to elaborate will often give us a more detailed answer that alleviates our concern. But when that doesn't resolve the issue, I'd encourage everyone to take a careful look inside. What's the point that seems objectionable? What message do you think you're hearing? How would you describe that type of offense? Maybe try completing this sentence: "I hate it when people…."

What's your earliest memory of a similar experience? Now, what can you do to alleviate that pain? Is there a part of you that fears the perceived message is true? Do you feel condemnation because you believe your own SELF-condemnation? If so, is that feeling based in reality due to an unresolved guilty conscience? Or is that feeling coming from condemnation unfairly heaped on you in your past? Or both?

I'm not suggesting you're imagining this current offense—I have no idea. But this analysis can give you long-term solutions and freedom from pain.

One reason for a premature hostile reaction is thinking the speaker belongs in a category that has already been rejected—a "wrong" political group, religious group, or whatever. In many cases, regardless of affiliation, the speaker's ideas at that moment are completely compatible with the listener's, even if the terminology is different: Words are just tools for conveying ideas. It's the IDEA that must be examined.

In the face of this premature rejection, the opportunity for a mutually beneficial alliance is lost. Fearful tribalism does not benefit anyone, and it goes against what Jesus taught, as he strongly rebuked judgmental attitudes. Likewise, in the Old Testament, we find this strongly worded message, Proverbs 18:13 in The Jubilee Bible: **"Whoever answers before listening is both foolish and shameful."**

Everywhere we go in today's world, we can find these fearful, knee-jerk reactions. They're a universal human problem, but we can work on that.

## *Self-Condemnation*

Sometimes we feel self-condemnation over the past. Some might tearfully say they know they should forgive themselves, but they just can't. They might even say they know God has forgiven them, but they still can't forgive themselves. It helped me to hear someone say that's actually the sin of pride: "You think you know better than God how to think about things. You won't relinquish control. You are trying to manage the universe rather than letting God manage the universe."

I thought that was a valid point, and it DID help me let go of self-condemnation. And yet, healing takes time. It's a challenge to rewire lifelong thought patterns. Thoughts are lightning fast! I still battle against wrong thinking at times. But now I'm faster at refuting those thoughts and getting those stress hormones down. And as time has passed, some anxiety or negative thinking has just gone away.

## *Deep Self-Hatred*

Another obstacle to personal growth is deep self-hatred and extreme insecurity. Compared to people only caught in self-condemnation, these people have become toxic. They condemn others, but they don't apply the same brutal standards to themselves. They can't face their own flaws, and they fail to admit a mistake. Or worse, some will issue an apology and say the right words, but it's just a manipulation to placate you for a while. Their words mean nothing.

**I think the refusal to face personal flaws is the #1 factor that destroys relationships. Some people can't accept themselves as flawed human beings. So they can't function in the context of reality. It takes two functioning human beings to make a good relationship.**

As a counselor, I've helped to restore a broken marriage, and I've seen a marriage reach a final collapse. The difference between success and failure was the willingness of the marriage partners to look at themselves and take responsibility. Period, full stop. The "blame game" fuels hatred:

> "You're the bad guy!"
> "No, YOU are the bad guy."

The antidote is for both people to WANT to examine their own flaws and mistakes and wounds. Once you understand that internal identity change, it's not only easier to do, but it becomes enjoyable. Yes! Learning and growing can become enjoyable!

*Arguing for Failure*

Have you noticed that some people habitually resist useful information? In ordinary conversation, I'm not the type to tell people what to do, but if they speak at length about their arthritic knee pain or troublesome thyroid or something else I've experienced and overcome, I might offer a "life preserver"—a single sentence mentioning what helped me with that same issue.

Even when I have spent time being a good listener, knowing that people need to vent and gain trust first, even then I see such people instantly reject that one-sentence life preserver. This is such a common human trait that we counselors are warned in our training to watch for it, and make sure we "don't work harder than the client." I call their reaction the "yeah, but" response: "Yeah, but I don't think that'll work because…." I also call this "arguing for failure." These people are determined to tell you why nothing can work and they'll stay miserable forever. Those of us who could be capable of helping eventually have to give up. But in my communication workshops, I teach techniques for getting past the "yeah but" response.

This issue deserves more thought from all of us, for everyone's sake. How much more suffering do we all want to experience?

Sometimes, when people start arguing their problem has no solution, they may even sound a little annoyed at us for not agreeing with them. We offer that one-sentence life preserver, and they hear that they could maybe solve the problem, if only they were willing to take action. That's the potential truth that inevitably accompanies a story of past success. But we'll often hear them respond, "No, nothing will work. It's genetic—there's no solution. That's just how it is."

What I sometimes do next is offer one more sentence. I might mention a YouTube video of a doctor presenting on that topic. But in the situations I'm describing, the response is clear: "Nope. Not listening." After my two separate sentences, I call it quits, and I secretly think to myself, *Okay. I did my part. My conscience is clear—I did not enable your misery. Now I must release you.*

How sad for them and their future suffering! Except that I refuse to let myself argue for THEIR failure. So I then think something more optimistic: *Maybe I planted a seed, and someone else will help that seed grow. Maybe they haven't hit bottom yet. Maybe they haven't become sick and tired of being sick and tired. We're playing a long game here. Let's not give up hope, but now, it needs to be someone else who will step in to play a role. Life is a team sport!*

I've been around the block enough to know that many people will recoil even at the thought of offering the two single sentences. Perhaps they fear offending or losing their popularity. So they just nod sympathetically and play the game that some call "Ain't It Awful." Let's all sit around and talk about how awful everything is. No wonder so many people feel depressed!

**Our challenge is to find a healthy middle zone, where we don't remain silent and promote human misery, but we also don't let that pendulum swing to the unsympathetic side.**

In these cases, I am not talking about someone just going through a hard time. Those people need strong sympathy and support. I'm also not talking about a situation where we've mentioned a possible solution, but others have MORE KNOWLEDGE than we do, and they kindly explain why that idea can't work for them. We must stay humble! Always ready to learn! This isn't about US and OUR comfort and OUR desperate desire to be rid of the issue with glib answers!

Can you see why this might be the most DANGEROUS idea I'm presenting in this entire book? I do not want any of us to become uniformly unsympathetic! That would be a crime against humanity, and one of the worst forms of hypocrisy. If we find ourselves saying things like, "I don't do pity parties," we should check ourselves to make sure we know how to be LOVINGLY PRESENT with people and give them support when times are tough. That ability to abide with people and correctly judge what they need requires emotional strength and spiritual discernment on OUR part!

**For the sake of our society, each of us should find this middle zone, this ability to sense the difference, this PLACE OF WISDOM.** Taking time for deeper relating seems to be a vanishing art in this culture, so let's take life more slowly. Then we'll be in a position to help by speaking up rather than shrinking back into timid people-pleasing. Our society has drifted into thinking it's not appropriate to challenge someone or express a concern. Let's examine this cultural trend:

> If you saw a friend about to step in front of an oncoming car, would you remain silent to save your popularity? Of course not. We would probably say that question doesn't make sense. So why has our culture descended to watching people self-destruct in other ways and saying nothing?

We won't let the pendulum swing to becoming a know-it-all, pushing ideas onto people or nagging. We're talking about love, wisdom, and gentleness. We're talking about maybe starting with, "I care about you, so I need to share the concern I have." We step out courageously to do the right thing when we're called to do so and the timing is right. We're willing to pay the possible price because we don't worship the idol of popularity.

Then maybe we let it go, depending upon the situation—how well we know people, how much influence we have, how serious the problem, and so on. We can even tell people right up front we're seeking a healthy middle zone—showing love and concern without inappropriate efforts at control. We can ask them to let us know if we missed the mark. We're all learning. We're all in this together.

### Denial and Uninformed Reasoning

Sometimes people find additional ways to argue and resist valuable information. Think of conversations about cigarette smoking, as one example. The science is clear that cigarette smoking is one of the worst things you can do for your health. But notice how some people react:

- silently—*Eh, I'm not gonna worry. I'll be fine.*
- or aloud—"My neighbor smoked like a chimney and lived to be 101!"

I assume you know the silent thought is foolish human denial or wishful thinking. Teenagers are known for thinking they're invulnerable, but we all tend to retain some of that trait. Even now, I catch myself reverting to that kind of thinking: *Should I eat this food or do this thing that could help my cancer return? Eh, it'll be okay.* I'm definitely guilty of this too. If we pay attention to what we eat, how often we exercise, and so on, we might realize we're engaging in this kind of denial on a regular basis!

As for the neighbor who lived to be 101, we need to give this more thought. **First, the rare exception does not disprove the general rule.** We must understand statistical risk. In science, truth is often a matter of mathematical odds, not absolute guarantees. If someone always hopes to beat the odds, we might assume that's a recipe for disaster. But also, we must examine those rare exceptions to see what we can learn, because they help us identify ALL the factors involved in good health.

### *Teenage Rebellion*

Some people—again probably due to emotional pain—are forever caught in what I call "teenage rebellion." They could be ANY age now, but in their 20s they should've started to realize their parents were right about some things. They should've stopped taking delight in being different from parents just for the sake of being different. They should've started to realize they DON'T know everything, as teenagers tend to believe. In the process of maturing and coming down to earth, they should have become willing to learn from others in general. As the saying goes, "A word to the wise is sufficient."

But if you're good at reading nonverbal communication, you can see that some people never seem to drop that "talk-to-the-hand" attitude. Here's a saying that applies to people like this: "Ya can't tell them nuthin!" They may think they're hiding their resistance, but it shows in their nonverbal behavior!

People in this category are similar to those who "argue for failure," but the resistance seems to come from more of an angry, oppositional childhood pain rooted in parental relationships, rather than a discouraged type of pain or learned helplessness or irresponsibility.

In the case of some men, this thing I call "teenage rebellion" stems from anger over being controlled by their mothers, where they've never become fully conscious of the problem and stood up for themselves. In the examples I've encountered, the unconscious thought that seemed to drive their behavior was, *Mother must be defeated at all times.* That's the demon they were forever fighting. The problem was they were fighting "mother" in the form of all other adults—a girlfriend, wife, coworker, an authority figure such as a boss, and so on.

People with this problem refuse to ACCEPT INFLUENCE. They will treat you as though you know nothing, have nothing valuable to offer. Research shows men with this problem are much more likely to get divorced, so we should never take this stubborn, demeaning trait lightly.

One of the worst examples I ever experienced went way beyond nonverbal behavior. The man put his fingers in his ears and laughingly howled at me an obscenity-filled comment designed to denigrate women and deliver this message: "I won't listen. I won't be influenced by you." And it wasn't during an argument. It was just a casual, lighthearted conversation.

But let's not demonize men, because not all of them are doing that! Instead, let's encourage more good men to step forward to teach other men how to be noble human beings, good husbands, and good fathers. To these good men we say, "We desperately need you.

Other men are hungry for your wisdom. Deep down, they WANT to be freed of their self-hatred."

**The failure to recognize and heal our pain from childhood is one of the greatest contributors to human misery! It's not weakness to acknowledge our pain. It's weakness to hide from it. Every single one of us must heed this saying: "You don't heal what you don't feel." You HAVE TO face your demons if you want a happy, healthy life. Anything else is cowardice and misery. Tough words, but true.**

I heard from one military retiree that the culture there has this expectation: *Act tough. Never admit you're struggling. Never admit to emotional wounds. Only weak, pathetic people need a counselor.* Given his age, I wonder if his criticism is now out-of-date, but regardless of what's true about today's military, I do believe that philosophy—wherever it might still exist in today's world—mirrors the ethos of the classic dysfunctional family: *Smile and act like everything's fine.*

People who promote this ethos might argue their case like this: "Counseling only perpetuates a victim mindset and creates a bunch of crybabies. These people need to take responsibility and pull themselves up by their bootstraps." I think there's a piece of truth in the idea of pulling ourselves up by our bootstraps, but GOOD counselors help us take responsibility, and they are trained to confront the client when necessary. Good counselors facilitate the most courageous quest of all—humbly facing our own humanity, flaws, and feelings. If you want to develop great leaders, there's your recipe.

Anyone who believes in stuffing feelings and pretending they aren't there fails to understand this law of the universe: If you try to suppress and shame negative feelings, they only grow stronger or morph into something worse. But if you allow them air, make space for honest recognition of the truth, and examine them in a healthy, Godly light, they start to die a natural death. As always, it's the pursuit of truth that counts, not maintaining a false persona.

A counselor could help people like the howling and laughing man identify old wounds and heal, but they have to be willing to learn. If they're truly stuck in "teenage rebellion," they're not teachable! Many times, these people have to hit bottom so hard they finally become desperate to consider ideas from others. Or maybe they find people who enable them, and they never change. And those enablers pat themselves on the back for "keeping the peace." Remember my comment about extreme conflict avoidance enabling evil?

### *The Avoidant Habit*

And then there are the avoidant individuals, but they're not all alike. Some are just incredibly uncomfortable with touchy subjects or conflict discussions, having learned to fear the outcome.

Some have a problem with GENERAL ANXIETY, but they blame their anxiety on other people. Chronic anxiety is estimated to be 30–50% genetic, and it could also come from living with an anxious-avoidant parent, trauma, microbiome issues, and more. Regardless of the origin, they've spent their lives trying to avoid challenges that heighten their anxiety. The more they avoid, the more cemented their avoidant habit becomes, and the more their anxiety grows. The tragedy is, if their chief coping strategy is avoidance, they're robbing themselves of the only way to grow stronger. The solution is to turn and face the monster, which in this case means getting help to face anxiety-provoking situations. Spiritual healing makes success possible.

Some avoidants have a deep mistrust of others—a damaged sense of trust overall—and think emotional intimacy is too frightening. They don't want to let themselves be known. So what began as a desire to avoid pain backfires, and then they see themselves as victims. They can't see that the problem began with their own avoidance, withdrawal, secretiveness, and dishonesty. A good relationship requires trust.

Some avoidants are angry and jealous of those who don't feel bound to the "religion" of avoidance. Their unconscious thought might be *I've lived this way my entire life, and you're showing me there's a different way of functioning? You must be doing bad things. I can't accept that I've been standing in a prison cell when the door was wide open all along!* In their anger, they might even cross into being abusive, as I experienced. Being angry and being abusive are two very different things, but sometimes they coincide. By the way, there IS such a thing as justifiable and righteous anger. Don't let anyone tell you anger is always a sin, or a forbidden emotion. It's your smoke detector, letting you know something needs fixing. That something could be inside of you, outside of you, or both.

### An Opposite Philosophy Rooted in Pain

Sometimes two people in a discussion have opposite philosophies, and both philosophies are valid. That's because the two of them are looking at different segments of the population or different aspects of life. If they can agree with one another that the opposite philosophy is also sometimes true, they are collaborating and correctly seeing the complexity of human life. But I couldn't begin to count how many times I've seen two people in an either-or argument. They mistakenly think only one is right.

Our national media have sometimes set a bad example with polarizing arguments, perhaps hoping to grab attention. The sound-bite either-or argumentation leads people to speak hastily, interrupt each other, twist the truth, or flat-out lie. Nobody wins in those conversations. Civil society just keeps declining. But other media personalities have found that people LOVE long-form discussion, where complex subjects are considered calmly, with no rush, and from multiple angles. So again we have the power: We can control our own conversations and our media viewing.

Here, "rooted in pain" means that sometimes people have seen a particular truth that brought tremendous pain and led to an obsession: *Not only do I know I'm right, but I'm fanatical about it. I have to have things a certain way or I'll panic. And I see this problem behind every rock! If anyone holds a different philosophy, I become alarmed and attack that individual's character.*

I suspect people with this trait don't realize what's happening in their own minds. If they are self-reflective, they will examine their panic. But one insight for the rest of us is that SOME people who launch ad hominem attacks aren't using them to win an argument with evil manipulation. Sometimes their response is a trauma response. This does not relieve them of the responsibility to calm down and listen to the other side, but it does help us to realize not everyone is purposely being malicious.

I hope that analysis gives you insight and helps you deal with others. As we learn and grow, we grant ourselves grace. As the saying goes, "Rome wasn't built in a day." Just "brick by brick."

One good move is to resign as self-appointed Manager of the Universe. I hope we can all laugh at ourselves over that human desire! We finally come to a place where we accept there's a lot we can't change. And I truly do mean ACCEPT. Knowing something intellectually and accepting it are two different things! With real acceptance, it does hurt less—eventually. There might be a deep grief at first. We might be letting go of our fondest dream or our most dearly beloved. But as we make our way through the grief process, we really do come to a place where we finally get some pain relief. As Robert Frost said, "The only way out is through."

**So the bottom line is to focus on what we CAN control, and the best place to start is with ourselves. There's great opportunity for progress there, and that's a wonderful, happy place to be.**

But there's also such a thing as INFLUENCE. I don't fully agree with the statement, "You can't change other people." I think it's true to a great degree, but I also know we're more likely to help others change if we give up our ATTACHMENT to changing them. One of those great ironies in life!

# *Body*

# 14

# The Origin of My Holistic Approach

It all began when I helped a boyfriend mow a farmyard at the age of 19. Prior to that, I had few significant health problems, except extreme nearsightedness and that strange "nausea" I mentioned earlier. But on this particular day, plodding along on that riding lawn mower through the grass and weeds, I knew I had been "over-exposed," for lack of a better term. Right away, I had severe allergy symptoms—runny nose, watery eyes, cough.

As I understand, allergies are an inappropriate reaction to a natural substance—it's not the substance that's the issue, but rather our immune system.[1] I now realize that chemicals my dad used in the construction of our house might have possibly done immune system damage.[2] Building materials, carpeting, and paint can also outgas toxic fumes, although some paints have improved.[3,4] I suppose emotional stress and the typical American diet had taken their toll. And I was in a generation of babies given cow's milk from the day we were born. That's not good for many reasons.[5]

So maybe I was a ticking time bomb, just waiting for that moment of overload.

After that, I was miserable. My allergies were so bad, if I sat outside on a spring day, I would look like I was crying my eyes out—tears rolling down my cheeks, mucous pouring out my nose. The occasional itchy throat and congested lungs added to my torture. Spring and summer were the worst, but I had problems year round. Some days, I had to take an antihistamine, but as you may know, those can zonk you out. It's not really living when you have to sleep to escape your misery.

This situation introduced me to the difference between allopathic medicine (what we here in the West think of as our "traditional" medicine) and functional medicine (a more holistic, naturopathic mind-body-spirit approach).

Generally speaking, the allopathic-traditional medical model is to wait until symptoms appear and then manage symptoms with drugs, surgeries, or other treatments—there is comparatively less effort to maximize overall health and address root causes of a problem.[6] Functional doctors and researchers, on the other hand, help you maximize your health by educating you about your body's biology and showing you what would be OPTIMAL in your lab tests, so that you can catch a problem early, perhaps decades earlier, when your pain and suffering will be much less.[7]

So taking an antihistamine was only treating symptoms. WHY did I have allergies? Back then there was no information, as far as I knew. But at least I could learn holistic strategies:

*Avoiding the Bad:*
- No carpet or other dust catchers such as stuffed animals or heavy draperies. They used to advocate vinyl roller shades for windows, but now we know more about toxic plastic fumes, so I opt for aluminum or real wood blinds.
- Vacuum cleaners and air cleaners with HEPA filtration to avoid recirculating the bad.
- No artificial fragrances in the home or in personal care products: They're allergenic hormone disruptors.[8]
- No mold, even old books that have that "old" smell.
- No toxins such as cigarette smoke, alcohol, car exhaust, herbicides, etc.

*Increasing the Good:*
- Healthy diet
- Exercise
- Quality sleep

If you're already familiar with holistic health or functional medicine, you'll notice that several strategies are missing from this list. Medical knowledge in the "developed" world was more limited back then. In the last few decades, scientific research has actually—believe it or not—started to catch up to ancient wisdom in advocating these important health strategies:
- "Taking every thought captive," avoiding negative thoughts and focusing on the positive.
- "Being transformed by the renewal of our minds," experiencing a change of identity. We're talking about literally becoming a new person: Researchers have seen changes in cells, biochemical reactions, brainwaves, genes, neurotransmitters, hormones, etc. Then our thoughts, behaviors, feelings, and energy also improve!
- The power of meditation and prayer to keep us connected and heading in the right direction.

- The power of acceptance and forgiveness to change everything, especially stress hormones.
- The power of SPEAKING positivity because "death and life are in the power of the tongue."
- The value of prevention over treatment.
- The value of banding together—"emotional support."
- The benefits of fasting.
- The power of both touch and belief for healing.

I'll stop there, but if you're into holistic health, you already know these ideas are gaining wider acceptance. They're transforming traditional medicine into "integrative" medicine, where some effort is made to combine the two medical worlds.

CUSTOMER DEMAND is helping to create these changes. Medicine is a business. Business goes where there is money to be made. So assuming you're not forced into a decision, THE POWER RESTS WITH YOU.

**And here's why this is so important for the purpose of this book: We need holistic strategies to feel good overall and to attack the root cause of illness, because it's hard to feel happy if we or our loved ones are exhausted, sick, or dying!**

To battle my allergies, I eventually went to an allergist and tested allergic to many things. But my absolute WORST allergy—the worst rating possible on a skin test—was grass! No surprise there. The allergist deserves credit for being more holistic, even back then. He provided educational handouts discussing the avoidance strategies I listed, plus a list of food additives to avoid:
- Aluminum found in baking powder
- Aspartame (NutraSweet, Equal, etc.)
- Preservatives and food colorings
- Gums and modified food starch
- Mono- and Diglycerides

- MSG—Monosodium glutamate
- Sodium nitrite and nitrate
- Sulfites

As a high school teacher, I learned more from a student who had rheumatoid arthritis so severe she couldn't walk up the stairs to my classroom. They sent her to a specially filtered and pure hospital, where every effort was made to reduce environmental toxins. She was told to bring only natural fiber clothing—either 100% cotton or 100% linen. They fasted her for six weeks, and she said they'd come in during those weeks, smell her skin, and say, "Nope, you still stink. We'll keep fasting you."

One thing she tested allergic to was corn. Her arthritis medicine had a corn base. But get this: After six weeks of fasting, she was completely arthritis-free! During her time there, they taught her all about nutrition. I will never forget her later standing at my desk and asking me, "Do you know what happens to your body when you eat a piece of apple pie?" The look of horror on her face certainly made an impression! Seems like they did a good job of educating her. And now, all these years later, the information is more widespread about the negative effects of sweets and other high-glycemic foods. Now we know how such foods disrupt human health and can influence everything from depression to Alzheimer's disease, dementia, diabetes, heart disease, cancer, and more.[9,10]

In fact, I recently met with a cardiologist because of the risk of heart damage from my cancer drug. During our visit, I playfully said, "So! What have you all decided is the cause of heart disease?"

He said, "It's the sugar." He went on to explain that excessive blood sugar creates the inflammation that causes arterial plaques to form.

How did they get that wrong all these years? For decades we were told saturated fat and cholesterol cause heart disease, and we were encouraged to switch our fat consumption to the industrial "vegetable oils," which are really pro-inflammatory seed oils.[11] Apparently, it's true that saturated fat can raise serum cholesterol, but some scientists now say high cholesterol alone is not bad when the other heart-disease risk factors are absent.[12] We're now hearing that systemic inflammation drives disease, and high blood sugar, among other things, causes inflammation.[13]

So what happened? Researchers have documented a long-term effort, partly suggested and funded by a sugar association, to hide the full truth.[14] And researchers have sounded the alarm about similar bias in research more broadly speaking: "Industry-sponsored nutrition research, like that of research sponsored by the tobacco, chemical, and pharmaceutical industries, almost invariably produces results that confirm the benefits or lack of harm of the sponsor's products, even when independently sponsored research comes to opposite conclusions."[15] The glycemic topic will reemerge later.

Considering my miserable allergies, you can probably see why I was motivated to take care of my health. I did a fairly good job by bureaucracy-advocated standards of the time. But I'll admit I didn't heed the warning of my high school student. I still ate desserts on many occasions. I also ate high-glycemic foods such as white flour pasta and noodles, homemade biscuits, pizza crust, waffles, bagels, and more, and I thought that was just fine. But now I know so much more, and I've been forced to take these matters seriously. If I had heeded the warnings of my high school student, I perhaps would have saved myself from cancer and more.

But I can't spend energy regretting the past. What's done is done. I try to focus on what I should do now, and that includes helping you.

# 15

# The Next Three Decades

Over the next three decades I had no health issues by traditional standards. I won't count the occasional cold or bronchitis, and I still had a better-but-not-gone case of nasal allergies. That meant my immune system was still not functioning correctly. But nobody back then seemed concerned about that, maybe because we didn't know as much. So during my next 30 years, according to traditional medicine and their standard lab ranges, I was healthy and everything was fine.

*Oh, those painful fibrocystic breasts? That's not really a health issue. That's just a natural thing, a "woman thing." Just take vitamin E and avoid caffeine. You'll be fine!* Vitamin E might have helped my symptoms, but now I know those alpha tocopherol capsules are a cheap, artificial form of vitamin E and only one of EIGHT types of vitamin E we should be getting from food. And I've seen reports that artificial alpha tocopherol sometimes shows no health benefit or might increase cancer risk.[16]

In this book I'm asking you to do your own research, so I need to prepare you for the challenge. As for me, I only look at PubMed, my own test reports, and other supposedly respectable sources. Then all I can do, as one ordinary citizen, is let others know what I've read. So this is a good time to warn you, for the sake of not only your happiness, but perhaps also your sanity! If you want to start looking at research to determine what is DEFINITELY TRUE, good luck! Some things are definitive and well understood. But if you start wading into health research, I think you'll soon encounter the following:

### Contradictory Opinions

It's amazing how many contradictory opinions are out there—on just about everything—and I've seen doctors GET ANGRY or MOCK another doctor who has a different opinion. But in those cases, from what I saw in the research, the agitated doctor was wrong.

The research articles themselves often generate opposite conclusions, as you now know.[15,17] I once heard an expert say, "If you see two well-designed studies with opposite conclusions, you can assume there's purposeful bias at play." He seems to be optimistic about our ability to create well-designed studies. Those are extremely expensive.

So why does anyone fund a study? Often it's because there's tremendous profit potential—the expense could be a good investment. The big and powerful can afford big studies, especially when politicians give them YOUR tax dollars. Meanwhile, solutions that could be more effective and less harmful, but would cut the profits of certain companies, might be ignored. Then on various websites you'll read, "There is no good scientific evidence that [this more natural or inexpensive substance] will help...."

Sometimes this would be a fair response: "Of course there's no research evidence if no one will fund the studies."

*Misleading Headlines*

I know of one case where researchers have been accused of purposely misrepresenting the truth regarding a more natural treatment for cancer. The accusation is they persist in studying the WRONG VERSION of that more natural substance so that they can advertise failure. Their headlines are basically announcing, "See? We told you it doesn't work!" But other researchers can see through that. One legitimate review says something like: Given the fact that it's well documented that [this substance] has to be in the XYZ form in order to work, it's interesting that some researchers persist in studying the ABC form and then proclaim it doesn't work.

I'm omitting the details because I don't want to send us down a rabbit hole. I just want you to be aware of the mistrust that's out there even among people in the profession. One former editor of a prestigious medical journal has been quoted as saying we can no longer trust much of the research or rely on our physicians and their guidelines. Another has cited problems with small sample size, bad analysis, and "flagrant conflicts of interest."[17]

If the goal is to make a profit, there's also the temptation to overstate the positive case for a drug in the headline and in the summary, but we must look at the data. Perhaps the drug only helped a certain type of patient—not all the patients in the study as the headline implies. The other patients might take the drug, suffer the side effects, but gain no benefit. And let's remember, not all side effects are mild and temporary. Some drugs can cause permanent organ damage![18]

Also, sometimes researchers only establish correlation—not cause—but the media run with headlines spreading false conclusions.

**But here's good news:** There is now research on the benefits of healthy foods for treating various health issues, in addition to prevention. And the analysis is deep into the "biochemical weeds." That means researchers have observed what happens at the biochemical level, so they have a good idea of WHY this food is helping you. Reading that can motivate you to eat healthy foods and can even add to the PLACEBO EFFECT, which is our name for the truth that whatever the human mind BELIEVES can have tremendous power to create positive change. Of course, Jesus was saying that two thousand years ago, but now we have scientific proof!

You can check research by searching: "PubMed health benefits of…" or "PubMed anti-cancer effect of…" and complete the phrase with the substance of interest. In addition, Dr. William Li's book *Eat to Beat Disease* summarizes some of this research. To access the biochemical weeds, see the studies at the back of his book. This holistic, natural side of medicine is exploding—see my website for my favorite resources.

As I explain these dangers, I want to emphasize I'm not commenting on ALL research. I've read research that gives me a deep feeling of awe and respect. We should admire the years of intense dedication and the brilliant communication skills evident in those writers! To me, reading one of THOSE reports is like watching a great moment in sports history or a stunning virtuoso musical performance—all we can do is marvel at what humans are capable of achieving! So to those scientists, THANK YOU!

Now that I've alerted you to some challenges in the field, let's continue.

One time, in my early 50s, I went to my GP for a bad cold, expecting to get antibiotics. (I didn't know even then how disastrous antibiotics are for the microbiome.) You can tell he hardly ever saw me, because he said to me, "Wow! A person over 50 and not on any medication! That's rare!"

I had always believed I wanted to avoid prescription medication as much as possible, preferring natural ways to maintain health. I'm sure my education about allergies got me started with that. Here's another example in which something "bad" in life leads to something good. I also had heard others say that taking a medicine to mask symptoms is like snipping the wire under the hood when your check-engine light comes on: You might avoid that red light, but the root problem will grow worse.

**The truth is, your tax dollars are funding symptom-masking drugs for multiple conditions, many of which could be eliminated FOR FREE with a healthy lifestyle! I hear the budget for medical care is now larger than our military budget, and predicted to grow—partly because Americans are being misled.**[19,20]

Well, during those three decades, according to traditional medicine, I was fine and there was NO NEED for pharmaceutical drugs. Oh, those painful fibrocystic breasts? Now I know that was a sign of "estrogen dominance," which means I had too much estrogen compared to progesterone, according to a basic definition in traditional medicine. Doctors who are more holistic explain that estrogen dominance can include a failure to correctly process and detox your natural estrogen, being contaminated with estrogen-like toxins such as pesticides, and failing to produce enough progesterone due to stress and poor diet.[21] And just yesterday, I heard a doctor say that 99.9% of the time an iodine deficiency is the root cause, because everything is so interconnected. An iodine supplement would've been an easy fix during all those decades, assuming he is correct. But basically my hormones were out of whack, and I was NOT HEALTHY!

Right here, I was going to write that it is "now understood" that excessive levels of NATURAL estrogen in the body, certain DOCTOR-PRESCRIBED sources of estrogen, and TOXINS that function like estrogen are all carcinogenic—and the general public is often not told that. But today I heard a doctor who claims to be campaigning for truth, and he insists there's no evidence that prescribed hormone replacement therapy (HRT) is carcinogenic.

Here's an example of the crazy back-and-forth I was talking about! We can suffer whiplash trying to follow all the conflicting science claims. I just have two thoughts for this doctor:

1. I guess somebody should tell the IARC—International Agency for Research on Cancer, part of the World Health Organization. They say HRT is indeed a Group 1 carcinogen.[22]
2. Speaking ONLY for myself, I believe it's best for me to avoid pharmaceuticals as much as possible and do my best to fix a hormone imbalance with proper diet, exercise, sleep, stress reduction, and other healthy habits. There's no substitute for taking care of myself, and I know healthy habits don't just eliminate one symptom—they create all kinds of benefits!

But my past ignorance about hormonal health left me with estrogen dominance for decades. Fast forward a few more years, and I get diagnosed with an estrogen-positive uterine cancer. I wish I'd had a functional doctor to help maximize my health rather than waiting for a cancer-catastrophe. But I'm getting ahead of myself!

# 16
## The First Major Crisis

Before the uterine cancer, I had to deal with another crisis, and I still am. It's called macular degeneration, a potentially severe loss of central vision as the center part of the retina—the macula—deteriorates and photoreceptors start to die. It's called "wet" macular degeneration when blood vessels start growing through the retina and leaking blood into the eye.

Here's an example of how traditional doctors have nothing to offer about root cause or helpful lifestyle habits. Yes, I know we can read online about the importance of a healthy diet, avoiding cigarette smoke and alcohol, and so on. But those articles don't offer adequate solutions, first of all. And secondly, I'm talking about what doctors would say there in the examination room. I have had eight different retina specialists in four different states, and none of them ever talked to me about lifestyle changes that could help, nor would they discuss root cause—except for one doctor who "made me cry," so to speak. I try to avoid the language of the powerless victim, but it's an expression I'll use this one time.

This was years into dealing with the situation and doing my own research. I had read in heavy-duty research the explanations for the damage to the retinas. I was intrigued to read a newer detail, that one of the factors was a reduction in the body of what's called the DICER1 enzyme.[23] So I asked this doctor his thoughts on that.

"We don't know what causes it." Period. End of comment.

I was flabbergasted. I tried to say something like, "But what about all those details I've read in the research?" How could he say we knew NOTHING? But he persisted. *Nope, nothing to see here, folks!*

To this day, I don't know if I fully understand WHY that upset me so much, but I remember sobbing to my friend about his behavior. *Was he really that ignorant? Could that possibly be?* It would be one thing for him to say, "Well, yes, we have this theory and that theory, but we're just not sure." I would've been just fine with that. But no! He refused to acknowledge ANYTHING! Even though I just said I'm not sure why I found his behavior so upsetting, I do have five parts to the answer:

**FIRST,** when something is such an important issue—WHO WANTS TO GO BLIND?—the stakes are high and the patient will naturally feel emotion.

**SECOND,** by denying the existence of the research I'd already read, it seemed he was undoing any progress. I was kind of excited about that DICER1 enzyme! And the doctors weren't going to help me, so I was trying to help myself! His denying the existence of that information felt awfully disheartening.

But here I must disagree with my own mind and how it was working back then. His OPINION doesn't have to make one bit of difference regarding what I should believe and what my solution path needs to be. That's one thing I learned from my cancer journey:

> *Doctors may SAY I'm going to die, but that's just an opinion based on a generalization after tabulating a massive number of people caught in a failing system. Even then, it was probably never true that 100% of them died. But either way, they have to admit they're a failing system, because they're predicting failure based on all their past failure! And probably most of those poor souls who died relied exclusively on that failing system rather than adding holistic strategies.*
>
> *So if the doctors have a failing system, WHY would I listen to a bunch of FAILURES when I'm pursuing SUCCESS? As the saying goes, "Those who say it can't be done should not interrupt those who are doing it." People in the business world understand this principle: You don't take business advice from people who have proven they don't know how to succeed. So too in the medical world! WHAT DO THEY KNOW? THEY'RE NOT GOD! Their opinion doesn't have to mean diddly-squat even if they are doctors!*

Remember my father challenging the wrong opinion of my fifth-grade teacher? What a gift he gave me! And I hope this book gives you that same gift. We all must learn to think for ourselves! Not in a stubborn way, but with an open mind and respect for the views of others. With humility, with an understanding of how complicated the human body is, combined with the spirit and the will to live. That's what I practiced during these years I call "my cancer journey."

So now I disagree with MYSELF as I reflect back on what I was thinking.

**Here's a tip: Don't hand the Doomsayers, the Negative Nellies, don't hand ANY of them the power to discourage you!** Easier said than done—believe me, I know! But you MUST do your own research, and then cling to both your knowledge and your faith. There are so many cases where doctors have been wrong we can't begin to count them all. But this tip applies not just to health issues, but to all of life!

**THIRD,** for someone like that doctor to DENY REALITY, that would be disconcerting to anyone who had researched as I had. But also I suspect it triggered my past trauma—being treated like I didn't know what I was talking about so many times in my life.

**BUT FOURTH,** it was more than that. We all look to doctors for help. To some degree, their presence can bring comfort, knowing we're not completely alone in this. Even if they can't solve our problem, we SHOULD have a compassionate human being to walk through the journey with us. There was something in his manner that suggested he ENJOYED denying the reality of the existing research. He seemed to ENJOY saying they don't know anything. With both his denial and the MANNER of his denial, he had stepped out of that supportive role, and I felt abandoned— probably touching another wound from my childhood.

**AND FIFTH,** this upsetting conversation occurred after years of researching macular degeneration, after years of living with the symptoms and the fear, and having just spent a year fighting cancer! (And just wait till you hear how THAT went!) This was also after OTHER deeply troubling experiences at the hands of doctors. And I had not yet found relief from some trauma. So I was pretty beat up emotionally at that point.

So that's my five-part analysis and maybe that's complete. But I don't know, because I don't know what I don't know. So now I'd like to use this example to challenge you just a bit, if you'll indulge me.

Can you think back to a time when someone was complaining to you as I did when I was crying to my friend? Can you think of a time NOT when it was easy to sympathize, but rather a time when you couldn't quite see it? Come on, we all have one, including me! You listened and you thought, *This person is making a mountain out of a molehill. It's not worth getting THAT upset!* You analyzed the supposed bad behavior. It definitely wasn't great, but it just didn't seem to merit this level of upset, right?

At this point I think we shift from judging the infraction to judging the person. And we conclude, *This person has a problem.* Then maybe a bit of superiority kicks in: *Thank God I'm not that sensitive!* Now, can you imagine listening to MY complaint—without knowing any of those five points? It's easy to be judgmental when we don't know the backstory, isn't it?

**So here's one other great tip: There's always a backstory! Be quick to listen, slow to judge, meaning DISCERN. We're not talking about being judgmental. That's something we should NEVER do.** To help with that, here's another thing we need to remember about human nature: We tend to have two sets of rules—what can upset US, and what should upset OTHERS. Most of us know this to be true. Hence this famous saying: "A recession is when your neighbor loses his job. A depression is when you lose yours!"

I see that as a comment on human nature—we can be awfully self-centered and unconcerned about other people's problems. We usually don't care as deeply until a problem hits us personally. Then suddenly the world is ending! Let's face it—that's often the way we humans are.

Strong parental love is an exception. The parental role should be all about abandoning selfishness and caring about our children as much as, and often more than, we care for ourselves. And we see other examples—heroes in battle, first responders. The world has LOTS of self-sacrificing heroes. Wouldn't it be great if more of us were like that on a more regular basis? We could all enjoy a more generous culture.

Stephen Covey, author of *The 7 Habits of Highly Effective People*, called the switch away from being judgmental a PARADIGM SHIFT. To illustrate, he told a story like this:

> A man is riding the subway and sees a younger man get on with several children. The children are rowdy, darting here and there, bothering the other riders. The man waits for the father to discipline them, but the father just sits staring at the floor. Irritated, the man approaches the father and says, "Sir, do you think you could control your children? They're bothering the other passengers!"
>
> The father seems to come out of his deep thought, looks around, and replies, "Oh, yes. We've just come from the hospital where their mother has died. I guess they don't know how to handle it."

Can you feel that switch from irritated judgment to sympathy? That's the power of a paradigm shift.

**So to recap, don't let others discourage you. When listening to others, remember that we don't know what we don't know—there's always a backstory. And let's try never to have two sets of rules—that's hypocritical.** One relevant video is Cleveland Clinic's "Empathy: The Human Connection to Patient Care." I think it's one of the greatest videos ever made.

### *Macular Degeneration in State #1*

When I was living in State #1, my left eye developed the "wet" form of the disease. I now realize it's likely that my wine consumption that year was a factor in my eyes growing worse.[24] I had been hanging out with wine drinkers, and I had that sense of invulnerability I described earlier. What a colossal mistake!

Doc #1 advocated a certain drug for injection. I did my research—all those drugs carried a risk of retinal hemorrhage, but the reported percent of patients was small. I don't know if there's a connection, but 18 months later, after driving through the mountains and experiencing that pressure change, I had a retinal hemorrhage—only in the treated eye. But it took me months to understand what had happened. It began as a dark cloud at the top of my vision. At my next exam, I tried to sound the alarm, but no one would listen to me. I gave up and didn't push. Big mistake.

**Macular Degeneration in State #2**

Three months later I moved to a different state, and 10 days after that, Covid shutdown! So there I was, all by myself, in a city where I hardly knew anyone. Day by day, the dark cloud was extending down the left edge of my vision. I researched online to learn what it could be and exclaimed aloud to myself, "Oh, my God! I think I've got a retinal hemorrhage!"

My first appointment with Doc #2 was weeks off, plus I felt hesitant to go in a crisis to a doctor I'd never seen before. So I made the long trip, at the beginning of the Covid shutdown, back to Doc #1. NOW he said he could see it. Why hadn't he noticed it before? That upper cloud was just as big the previous time, three months earlier. He advocated doing nothing, so I made the long trip back to State #2. Doc #2 suggested an immediate injection with a different drug to stop the bleeding and try to save my eyesight. That did seem to help, but after all those months of delay, scarring had formed, and vision was reduced.

## Macular Degeneration in State #3

Six months later, I moved again. Doc #3 was similar in personality to Doc #1—not warm or friendly. And here's how the next injection went: I felt the needle go in despite the use of a numbing agent. I could tell he went in deeper and with more force than previous doctors, and then BOOM! I completely lost vision in that eye, like I had no eyeball at all. He had already rushed out of the room as these doctors typically do, but I expressed alarm to the tech. She immediately dismissed my concern as meaningless: "Oh, that happens a lot."

"It's never happened to me before!"

"Just sit for a few minutes. It will come back." She was right. After many minutes, my vision in that eye returned. *BUT WHAT WAS THAT?* I now know the loss of vision could've come from the sudden increase in eye pressure because of the injected fluid, plus one other thing—hold that thought.

Fast forward to Doc #4. I mentioned my "macular holes," which are pits in the center of each retina. He angrily jumped on my comment: "You don't have a macular hole!"

I was stunned, trying to figure out what he could possibly mean, because I knew I DID. We went back and forth another sentence each, and then I recalled the full name was "LAMELLAR macular hole." So I gave him the full name, and then he conceded that yes, I did indeed have those.

Maybe he was distinguishing between that specific kind of hole and other types of macular holes, but there was no need to bite my head off. Did he think I was a retina specialist who knew all the other kinds? And would he have been that rude to a fellow doctor, if the doctor had lazily used a shorter name? **Do patients deserve respect or not?**

I felt like crying. After he was gone, I sniffled my way through checkout and started asking around for recommendations for a new doctor. Friends suggested Doc #5 at the same clinic, but I knew some clinics discourage you from switching doctors. They assured me it would be fine. So I called the office and said I wanted my next appointment to be with Doc #5.

The nice lady on the phone inquired as to why I wanted to switch. I hesitated but then said, "Well, I'm not interested in criticizing anyone but I was not happy with the way I was treated."

The woman was very kind and encouraged me to tell her what had happened. She profusely apologized, said I never should have been treated that way, and she'd be doing something about the situation, and of course I was welcome to switch.

So! Doc #5 was much better. Both polite AND competent. And then he gave me some bad news:

"You've got a retinal tear."

"A tear? What's that from?" I asked.

"A needle," he said.

*Oh.* Well, first of all, I appreciated his telling me. *An honest doctor!*

Have you figured out where the tear came from? I don't know, but due to the force of the injection and the immediate blindness, I think maybe it was Doc #3. At that point there was nothing to be done, and I was stuck with more visual distortion. Then I was diagnosed with uterine cancer. After a round of cancer treatment, I moved to yet another state.

### Macular Degeneration in State #4

Now we've caught up to the doctor who denied there were insights coming from research—Doc #6. Even though I gave a five-part analysis of why I was upset, I hadn't yet told you about the doctor who reacted angrily because I didn't use the precise term for my macular holes, and I hadn't yet told you about getting my retina hooked with a needle.

**So here's another tip: Even after you've heard a backstory, don't assume you've heard the WHOLE backstory.** In life, we usually don't take time to SHARE completely, and others usually don't take time to LISTEN completely.

I bet you can guess what happened after that upsetting conversation with Dr. Knows Nothing. Yep, I switched to a different clinic. Did things get better? No! Get ready for the most horrific experience of them all!

Well, maybe it's debatable whether this upcoming experience is worse than getting your retina hooked with a needle. Hmmm. I'll let you decide. Here's what happened:

I had seen a few good online reviews for Doc #7, so I was hoping for a nice guy. Nope, definitely not warm and friendly. He was probably in his 50s, stocky, with a rigid, stern, and gruff personality. I met him briefly, but this clinic, unlike the others, had a physician assistant who asked me to accept an injection from her. I usually lean toward cheerful optimism, so I looked her in the eye and said good-naturedly, "Well, I don't know. Do you have a steady hand?" She smiled and said she thought she did.

"Okay," I smiled back. And you know what? She did a good job, better than a few of those doctors. I saw her again the next month.

During the third visit, Dr. Gruff came in and didn't ask but TOLD ME I'd have a student do my injection.

*Oh, no! After everything I've been through, I'm drawing the line. PA, fine. But student? No! Not for sticking a needle in my eye. Go practice on patients who don't already have plenty of eye damage!*

I told him I did not want a student. Didn't I have the legal right to refuse? Surely I did, because they had asked my permission for the PA and a PA is already done with school and licensed! Here's where things got ugly. He said, "YOU HAVE TO!" But I stood my ground.

He seemed to let me win that argument, and then a strange thing happened: He came toward me with the needle, but rather than staying on my left side, to inject into my left eye, he crossed behind me and stood on my right. This is difficult to describe, but he held the needle in front of my face in a way that seemed fake, and he told me to turn my head even further to the right. As I did so, I heard someone move in on my left. Then the worst, most painful injection I had ever received!

Trust me on this—if someone is going to stick a needle in your eye, YOU KNOW NOT TO MOVE! But the pain was so bad, I jerked and yelled "Ow!" The needle was out. I never looked to my left—I was too focused on complaining to the doctor, saying that was the most painful injection I had ever received.

Dr. Gruff must now be renamed. We'll call him Dr. Nazi, because his response was to tell me that no, it WASN'T the most painful one I had ever had. Then he told me IT DIDN'T HURT!

Remember when we talked about gaslighting? An especially evil form of lying—the perpetrator is saying, "No, don't believe your senses. You DIDN'T experience what you just experienced." It's an assault on our rights and our sanity! And what's worse, people usually gaslight to try to get away with SOME OTHER evil behavior.

After that he was gone. I told the tech this was an outrage, that he had no right to tell me it didn't hurt, I know whether or not it was the worst shot I'd ever had—AND IT WAS—and he had no right to tell me what I'd experienced. I told her I wanted the PA for my next visit. But once I had time to think, I realized I could not return to Dr. Nazi's clinic. Not only was that a horrible experience, but also I could not trust what would happen during any future visit.

So back to the other clinic I went. Due to scheduling, they gave me a different doctor, Doc #8. The only significant thing was, he said the shots weren't doing me any good, so I might as well not have them!

That's an odd thing to say, because the stated purpose of the shot was twofold: 1) stop bleeding and blood vessel growth through the retina if needed, or 2) just prevent future blood vessel growth. I seemed to be gaining the preventative benefit, so I've often wished I had asked him what he meant—maybe just that my eyes were stable enough that the risk/reward ratio had shifted, considering all possible side effects of injection. At the time, I was just happy to escape the shots.

**UPDATE:** Recently—more than two years later—my OTHER EYE developed the wet macular degeneration. I received a shot with a different drug and three days later had a massive retinal hemorrhage that has destroyed my vision. I mean I can't see two fingers in front of that eye.

I alerted the doctor immediately but was told to wait three or four weeks for a recheck. At that point, the doctor referred me to a surgeon. The consultation date—not even the surgery—would be more than three months later. I questioned the delay and as a result of pushing, got there two weeks later, which was six weeks post-hemorrhage.

That's when the surgeon told me the surgery should've been done IN THE FIRST 7–10 DAYS for optimum results, and now there's virtually no chance for improvement. She claimed no one had told her the reason for my visit.

After that, I had to fight the bureaucracy at the local clinic to get treatment for my remaining eye, which used to be my "bad" eye. And when I finally got in there and asked how they'd monitor my healing, the tech scolded me for CAUSING TROUBLE BY ASKING QUESTIONS! To quote my oncologist, who heard about this, "Our medical world is so broken."

And just wait till you hear my cancer story!

# 17

# From Eye Problems to Cancer

If you look back, you'll see I was diagnosed with uterine cancer in State #3. But I prefer to start the numbering over and call that "Cancer State #1." If that seems confusing, I'd say don't worry about getting the details of my life straight—it's not really about me. It's about helping you! In this entire book, I'm just trying to alert you to ideas that you can research or ponder for yourself.

You might be tempted to assume you'll never have macular degeneration, although the numbers for chronic disease and macular degeneration specifically are increasing significantly.[25] **But experts predict one of every two or three Americans will have cancer at some point, and the numbers among younger Americans are rising dramatically.**[26,27,28] **You need to consider this information BEFORE you or your loved ones get diagnosed!**

About four years before my uterine cancer diagnosis, I was diagnosed with a bit of skin cancer on my forehead. It was removed and that was it. I never thought much about it. I should have, though, from a functional perspective. If your body's immune system can't eliminate cancer cells, or if you have "pre-cancer cells," that's not good from a functional perspective. In fact, come to think of it, I also had a bump with pre-cancer cells removed from my leg several years before that! The warnings are there for many of us.

**Please don't do what I did and ignore those signs. Don't be influenced by any doctor who might be slow to think systemically and sound the alarm!**

We have to start the cancer story by talking more about my macular degeneration, because everything is INTERCONNECTED. This doesn't surprise you, does it?

Here's an idea I think you'll want to embrace instantly: Everything to do with the human body is amazingly interconnected. Functional medicine understands this and is trying to treat the WHOLE person. You think your gut issues have nothing to do with your depression, which has nothing to do with your thyroid, which has nothing to do with your achy joints? Guess again.

Now from a more functional perspective, let's look at several factors that perhaps contributed to my uterine cancer. But first, we need to talk about the word "cause." I went looking for a single, official definition in the medical field. I'm not sure there is just one. Maybe that helps to explain all the arguing.

I checked the IARC, and they say a Group 1 carcinogen shows "sufficient evidence of carcinogenicity in humans." They determine that through epidemiological studies, animal studies, and strong evidence in humans exposed to that particular substance.[29]

I still wonder what numerical increase in risk is considered ENOUGH to say, "Yes, we see causality." I don't know what they do with the margin of error in all those studies. And I don't know if they try to weed out the biased studies.

Some people try to use an EXTREME definition of carcinogen: A substance that all by itself is GUARANTEED to produce cancer AND there must be proof with humans, not just animals.

That's the definition that probably leads someone to argue that the chain-smoking 101-year-old is proof that smoking doesn't cause cancer. They seem to think the word "cause" carries an absolute guarantee. The IARC explanations show we don't need a guarantee, just higher risk. Another problem with that extreme definition is that it's sometimes ethically problematic to wait for proof using humans because we try not to subject humans to dangerous substances unless absolutely necessary.

Here's a real-life example of confusion over this word "cause." I heard a registered dietician tell a group of cancer patients, "There's no evidence that sugar causes cancer." Was she correct only according to that extreme definition? To put it another way, is there proof that, if a person eats high-glycemic food long-term, we can COUNT ON that person developing cancer?

I don't think we can count on that. But is there proof that, if a person eats high-glycemic food long-term, that person is at INCREASED RISK of developing cancer? I think that's a solid yes: I'm confident a higher risk of some size is there, and I hear from cancer researcher Thomas Seyfried the proof is there.

So here's a tip for avoiding arguments. Notice we're simultaneously considering two ideas:

1. What's the truth?
2. What has the bureaucracy done to establish and communicate the truth?

If we examine each idea separately, we might have a better chance of finding answers. Rest assured I would never trust the word of a single researcher, so I turned to the National Institutes of Health. I urge you to read this study, "Nutrition and Cancer: A Review of the Evidence for an Anti-Cancer Diet," but elsewhere, the NIH reports that the evidence is inconsistent from one study to another.[30]

I say, given what we now know about the politics and bias in research, especially with high-glycemic food, the presence of inconsistency in research should not mean much. As the saying goes, "Fool me once, shame on you. Fool me twice, shame on me." Didn't we go down this road with heart disease? Is someone hoping we'll do it again with cancer?

Based on listening to countless doctors and researchers, I now believe ALL "lifestyle diseases" or "chronic diseases" generally stem from the same few causes, and a high-glycemic diet is perhaps #1 on that list, along with a lack of exercise, consumption of all vegetable oils, toxins, stress, and other factors.

When we use the phrase "lifestyle disease" or "chronic disease," we're referring to cancer, heart disease, stroke, type 2 diabetes, pre-diabetes, insulin resistance, metabolic syndrome, obesity, dementia, Alzheimer's, and perhaps depression, macular degeneration, and more.

**We don't have to wait for the entire bureaucracy to admit to the truth. We can improve our diets and exercise now! But please check with your doctor and exercise trainers to be sure of what's right for you.**

In an earlier draft of this book, right here I presented some of that evidence for the connection between a high-glycemic diet and cancer. I was summarizing more details from the NIH and other sources. But I started to feel exhausted, and I started to feel sorry for you having to wade through all that. I reached one of those breaking points I mentioned in my first chapter. I said to myself:

**"No, I'm not doing this anymore!"**

I've had it with the endless questions generated by my obsessive drive to get to the truth. Which sources are saying what? Based on what evidence? Which TYPES of cancer are they mentioning? Oh, only five or six types? What about all the other kinds of cancer? What about THIS kind of cancer or THAT kind of cancer? And what about the different "histologies" within each cancer type—what if the cancer is highly estrogen positive? Or not at all estrogen positive? What about progesterone positive or HER2 positive or PD-L1 positive?

Then there's the quibbling over "significant" and "non-significant." And what exactly is the difference between "moderate risk" and "borderline risk"? What if the authors of the article don't want to say the "C word," but they admit that a high-glycemic diet causes insulin resistance, and then pre-diabetes, and then full-blown diabetes, and elsewhere we find the evidence that all of that creates higher risk for cancer?

HOW MUCH DIGGING DO WE HAVE TO KEEP DOING?

Have you ever felt that the bureaucracy likes to play "rope-a-dope"? That was boxer Muhammad Ali's term for misleading his opponent up against the ropes and then wearing him out to secure the victory. We can definitely be worn out by trying to examine the available evidence. So I decided to spare you all that and removed that section. You already know I encourage you to do your own digging. The bottom line is there IS enough evidence to say Thomas Seyfried was right: **The evidence suggests the high-glycemic nature of our modern diet is contributing to cancer risk.**[30]

Regarding that endless debate about the word "cause," my simplified view after all these years is that cancer and other lifestyle disease—as well as good health—are all influenced by a combination of factors, so even if you take a "borderline" risk factor and add it to a few others, you can create a disaster in the body. And that's easy to do with our modern lifestyle.

I don't know about you, but I've seen enough, and I won't waste one more minute of my life quibbling with anyone over the intricate details in the research. **Not doing this anymore!**

So back to our registered dietician! She may be correct that there's no proof that sugar "causes" cancer all by itself. But for her to then suggest—which she did—that the cancer patients sitting there don't have to worry about foods that spike their blood sugar? I'm sure my stress hormones skyrocketed, because I felt she was endangering the lives of those patients—I know there's evidence for that. Here are three highlights:

1. We start with the idea just covered that chronically elevated blood sugar HELPS to cause cancer.
2. It's well known in medicine that cancer cells LOVE sugar. That's how a PET scan works: Compared to normal cells, cancer cells preferentially gobble up sugar, so they inject you with radioactive glucose, the cancer cells gobble it up, and the radioactivity makes tumors show in the imaging.
3. There is plenty of evidence to suggest that people who already have cancer are wise to avoid foods that spike their blood sugar. The pharmaceutical and supplement industries are MAKING MONEY selling products to cancer patients that lower blood sugar. So why would you spend money on those drugs or supplements and suffer the side effects, but then sabotage your progress by eating high-glycemic food?

I'm not suggesting the RD was TRYING to endanger cancer patients. I suspect it's more likely she's misinformed because she's an unwitting tool of the agri-food industry as they seek to protect their industry.

Let me hasten to explain that, ordinarily, I would have assumed she was just a poorly educated professional, but I started to form my suspicion only because she ALSO argued that genetically modified organisms (GMOs) are safe. If I could only use that extreme definition of the word "cause," knowing there's not yet much research on humans, I would not try to argue with her. But because I was so alarmed by her stance on sugar, which I saw as misleading, I did some quick research on GMOs.

Prior to that I had no opinion, had only heard random talk about avoiding them, but didn't know why. Now I'll point you to this study, which surveyed all literature and found 203 animal studies and one human crossover trial. They note that the serious adverse events include "mortality, tumour or cancer, significant low fertility, decreased learning and reaction abilities, and some organ abnormalities."[31]

I just heard someone in a podcast defend GMOs as being the same as hybridization, but it seems that is false—unlike a hybrid, the GMO is a laboratory creation that cannot occur within the laws of nature, and I'll point you to this study, which gives an explanation of all the potential risks—not just to human health, but to the entire ecosystem and also the worldwide economy: "Genetically modified foods: safety, risks and public concerns-a review." Articles like this show the urgent need for all of us to become educated.[32]

Some sources state that GMO plants also promote cancer because they're sprayed with the herbicide glyphosate. One of my medical test reports definitively states that glyphosate is carcinogenic, but so far as I know, the IARC has only classified glyphosate as "probably carcinogenic to humans."[33] And you probably aren't surprised to hear there's tremendous controversy.

**BUT HERE'S MY REAL POINT:** It's really a distraction to get lost in all the research on high-glycemic foods and GMOs. People who might want to confuse us can use endless scientific debates to their advantage. Like Muhammad Ali's "rope-a-dope."

My real question is this: Why is a registered dietician arguing in favor of sugar and GMOs? Why did she even need to go there? Call me a cynic if you wish, but I think we need to ask that question. To put it another way: Why did a HEALTHCARE PROVIDER encourage people to consume questionable substances, especially when they're already struggling with a life-threatening illness?

I don't know. But I gather from what I've read that some reasons for creating a GMO, beyond increasing crop yield, are increased corporate control of food production, in addition to increased revenue for the agri-food industry.[34,35] So maybe here are the next questions worth asking: What would happen to the agri-food industry if we all turned to natural, unprocessed foods? And what would happen to the pharmaceutical industry if people became healthier due to diet change and other healthy habits?

Just asking. And just picturing some lives saved. Did you know the estimate for 2025 cancer death is over 618,000 American men, women, and children?[36] And as you know, there are other chronic diseases that kill or destroy your mind. So I'm also picturing all those friends and family members who wouldn't have to grieve the loss of a loved one. And I'm thinking about the billions or trillions of tax dollars that could be diverted from medical costs to paying down the national debt and HELPING PEOPLE.

This is doable, folks! Is our junk food worth all this pain and suffering?

# 18

## Cancer Factors?

Now that we've covered the word "cause," I'll list what I have chosen to call my possible "cancer factors." In this entire book, I'm not trying to PROVE something to you. That's quite the challenge in the field of science—even for the scientists themselves, as you now know! Instead, I'm telling you about my search for answers, sharing what I've read, raising questions, and offering personal theories or opinions. Then you can do your own research, develop your own opinions, and make your choices.

I have tried to document carefully many of the more general medical topics covered so far. Now, as I transition to my more specific experience, I must move more quickly and not try to document everything I've read in the last four years of cancer research, plus the five years before that, trying to solve macular degeneration. I simply can't take time to duplicate nine years of locating and reviewing all that research. Instead, I must ease the burden on my eyes, as I'm sure you can understand, and I must also, for the sake of fighting cancer, avoid being too sedentary, sitting at my computer.

### *Cancer Factor #1?*

About nine years ago, when first working on macular degeneration, I consulted a naturopathic doctor who wanted me on a general vitamin pill—sold by her, of course. When I looked at the ingredients, I thought, *Huh. She must not know the research on macular degeneration. This pill includes the antioxidant* **beta carotene**, *but they took beta carotene out of the AREDS eye pill formula for triggering lung cancer in former smokers.*

This was back when I had more trust in medical professionals. I was COMPLIANT, because I had not yet learned the hard way that I had to think for myself. I told myself, *Oh well, I'm not a former smoker, so I should be okay.* In addition to my healthy diet, which had plenty of beta carotene, I started taking the pills.

Six months later I went to my dermatologist for a skin cancer recheck. No skin cancer, but she looked at me and said, "You're yellow! Back off the beta carotene!"

"I am?" I said. I couldn't tell. But she had the expert eyes.

Four year later, after I was diagnosed with uterine cancer, I came across an obscure article listing two lesser-known factors in creating uterine cancer—a sudden increase in beta carotene intake or a sudden increase in lycopene. I never took lycopene in pill form. But now you know about the beta carotene.

After the cancer diagnosis, I learned from a functional genetic test that my body is especially bad at converting beta carotene into the essential form of vitamin A that is stored in the liver. I have read that none of us can convert 100% of the beta carotene we consume, and the conversion ratio varies widely across our population. But many of us have this genetic condition that makes conversion even worse, and that can lead to more than turning yellow: Beta carotene can build up to toxic levels, and there's a correlation with both hypothyroidism and diabetes. My genetic report advised me to eat liver or egg yolks to get the genuine vitamin A.

Now, almost four years after the uterine cancer diagnosis, I've seen articles mentioning MORE types of cancer associated with beta carotene, even in non-smokers, and a different article warns of the correlation between a vitamin A deficiency and several kinds of cancer, including gynecological cancers! I spent my life not knowing all this, and I was only tipped off thanks to a genetic test ordered by a functional doctor.

But rather than running the whole population through genetic tests, maybe we just ought to warn people to eat animal sources of vitamin A to play it safe. I don't know about your nutritional needs, but for myself, I have calculated I only need about 1/2 ounce of liver per day to get sufficient vitamin A. That's a chunk the size of a postage stamp. You should also know it's important not to overdose on vitamin A. I keep the cooked chunks in the freezer and pop one in my mouth each day. But what I really should do is monitor my actual serum vitamin A level to see what I'm absorbing into my bloodstream. And I would need to research how reliable that test is—different substances leave the blood stream and enter the organs at various speeds, so sometimes it's hard to know what a blood test is showing. I have not done all that analysis.

In addition to the concern about vitamin A deficiency and cancer, I suppose you know which organ is most famous for using vitamin A? The eyes.

Do you see the problem? Experts say traditional doctors—including oncologists—are about 17 years behind the research. It takes at least that long for new research to filter down to doctors and the guidelines they follow. And as we probably all know, traditional medical schools generally don't give proper attention to nutrition and natural, inexpensive remedies. IT'S THE SYSTEM THAT NEEDS TO CHANGE.

*Cancer Factor #2?*

By naming this factor, I might be on the cutting edge of science. We'll see if future research validates my theory. I suspect another factor in creating my cancer was **the TOTAL number of antioxidant supplements** I took in hopes of fighting macular degeneration.

We've probably all heard of antioxidants, and back then I thought *more is better*. That's because when reading about macular degeneration, I was led to believe that reactive oxygen species molecules (ROS) were the enemy and had to be stopped with antioxidants. But after more research, I think I understand the body also needs oxidative processes to fight cancer. I now have notes saying that my kind of cancer can be inhibited by the blockade of two enzymes through ROS, but antioxidants disrupt that blocking action!

Certain antioxidant supplements are promoted as cancer-fighters, but my deep dive into the research reveals we're playing with fire, because if we don't get the dosage exactly right at the right time, we can FUEL cancer! I'm also reading that antioxidant supplements could POSSIBLY cause mitochondrial damage, which is now considered the root dysfunction for all chronic disease. Maybe the safest plan is to obtain antioxidants only from an extremely healthy diet.

### Cancer Factor #3?

Another factor was probably **an iodine deficiency and resulting hypothyroidism**. I just mentioned hypothyroidism linked to beta carotene! Hypothyroidism usually involves low levels of T3 and T4 thyroid hormones. Iodine is necessary for the synthesis of T4 and T3. But if we don't eat plenty of seafood or seaweed, don't consume iodized salt, or don't eat foods grown in iodine-rich soil, we can develop a deficiency.

The TSH lab test is how some doctors check the thyroid. The pituitary gland creates more TSH—thyroid stimulating hormone—when it senses low levels of thyroid hormone, but I had a high TSH with normal T3 and T4. A doctor trying to help me with my eyes looked at the TSH and said I was old, my thyroid was failing, and I should hurry onto thyroid medicine.

I told him I wanted to be a Sherlock Holmes and see what I could figure out by changing my diet. He agreed and said we would recheck the levels in six weeks. After only four weeks, I knew I was much better. My symptoms of fatigue and joint pain were gone. I rushed out and got a TSH test at my own expense. Sure enough, my TSH was back down. I now know we shouldn't rely on the TSH test alone to examine thyroid health. But in only four weeks, I made a drastic improvement by changing my diet. And now I know a simple iodine deficiency can harm my biochemistry, which might lead to cancer.

**UPDATE:** One of my functional doctors just told me the prescribed synthetic T4 thyroid hormone is carcinogenic. I checked and apparently some studies do show increased risk.

*Cancer Factor #4?*

Another factor was probably **elevated blood sugar**. I was sticking to a "healthy" Mediterranean diet with seafood, chicken, fruits and veggies, beans and lentils, and only whole grains because I was battling macular degeneration. But because I wasn't diabetic, in my ignorance I thought I could eat all the fruit I wanted. Same with grains and beans. I was trying to help my eyes with a massive consumption of foods rich in vitamins and minerals. But now I realize I should not have been eating a whole plate full of mango chunks! Or four bowls of oatmeal!

I even saw proof I was suffering from blood sugar elevation when one set of labs showed I suddenly had high triglycerides. Some quick research gave the answer: I had started to eat dates. Sure enough, once I quit eating dates and backed off other high-glycemic foods, my triglycerides were back down.

But now I suspect I had elevated blood sugar for too long. Higher blood sugar creates inflammation. Inflammation creates disease.

*Cancer Factor #5?*

Another possible factor is that my mother was given a powerful estrogen-like hormone called **DES** to try to stop a miscarriage two pregnancies before me. She lost that baby, so the drug didn't even work. But I believe the hormone remained in her body to some degree, because I was born with a malformed uterus and double cervix. It's well known that DES daughters can have a malformed uterus and be prone to cancer. The IARC has labeled DES a Group 1 carcinogen.

Some doctors and researchers might claim the DES would not have affected me, because I was not in utero when the drug was given. I think they had better read more research. I've read that DES is five times more powerful than the Estradiol form of estrogen, which is also known to be carcinogenic. I've also read that mouse studies have shown DES can cause problems not just for the daughters—the second generation—but even down to the THIRD generation! If DES can impact the third generation in mice, it seems reasonable to wonder if it can affect a human child born from that original mother's body, especially when a malformed uterus is evident.

The story of DES is even more worrisome, because sources say farmers were putting DES into the feed of nearly all cattle in the 1950s and 60s, until it was finally banned in 1972. If you think that's ancient history and the risk to you is negligible, you should know that the use of growth hormones continued to be an issue in U.S. meat production even after 1972. In 1989 the European Union banned the importation of U.S. meat containing U.S.-approved growth hormones, including a form of Estradiol. So what's the situation now? If you eat factory-farmed meat, I suggest you look into it.

The DES topic will resurface with my story of Dr. Nazi #2!

### Cancer Factor #6?

The double cervix creates a sixth factor. The literature occasionally states that **atrophied tissue** is a cause of my type of uterine cancer. For years I had to pay for two PAP smears because I had a double cervix. But in more recent years, as I was moving from state to state and warning gynecologists they'd see a second cervix, I started to hear, "I don't see a second cervix."

And I'd say, "Well, I know it's there. I've been paying for two PAP smears for years!" They acted like they didn't believe me, but now I think the cervix that had never been involved in childbirth—which was off to the side and perhaps the more abnormal cervix—had atrophied, and that's why they weren't seeing it. If I knew then what I know now, I would've had a hysterectomy to try to save myself from a cancer nightmare.

But again, no one is telling us these things because doctors don't know the research in their field. Shouldn't they? That's often what makes the difference between life and death.

*Cancer Factor #7?*

Another factor for adding fuel to the already existing "cancer fire" was my use of **hormone replacement therapy (HRT)** about six months before I was diagnosed. The HRT was another attempt to help my eyes. You probably know by now I'd be reluctant to use ANY pharmaceutical hormones, even bioidentical. Estrogen is generally understood to drive cell growth. While it is needed for reproduction, it's also a dangerous carcinogen when not processed correctly, in the correct forms—more information I didn't know.

When this doctor suggested the HRT, he never gave me any warnings. I did research but not enough. I only read that women who are ten or more years post-menopausal should not start HRT. The source did not say WHY. Because I was just past the ten-year mark, I questioned the pharmacist extensively. But again, I was too trusting. I was told I could start at half the dose if I had reservations. So I gave it a try.

In less than two months my breasts were so sore I rushed to the gynecologist for a mammogram and sonogram, always fearful of breast cancer. They saw no reason for my pain and suggested it was from old scar tissue. But this misery had developed in just the last two months! The doctors seemed clueless, but I knew: It was the HRT. I immediately dropped it and then bam! The uterine bleeding started. But the breast pain went away quickly. Figuring I had created an artificial menstrual period with that sudden drop of hormones, I was not alarmed and saw no need to rush to the doctor. Colossal, colossal, colossal mistake!

*Cancer Factor #8?*

**Emotional stress** hurts the gut microbiome and thus the immune system, and it elevates blood sugar to prepare for fight-or-flight. We don't need constant relaxation—handling a challenge produces healthy neurotransmitters, and wise exercise is "good stress." But chronic stress is a problem.

Relaxation, on the other hand, lowers stress hormones and blood sugar. I've tested my blood glucose with a Keto-Mojo, which measures glucose and ketones from a finger prick: After only 20 minutes of breathing and relaxation, my glucose dropped from 96 to 86. I have also used a CGM—continuous glucose monitor—which measures interstitial fluid and can give different results compared to the blood test. But during an easy 30-minute post-meal treadmill walk, I watched my glucose drop from 143 to 82, checking every few minutes—dropping, dropping, dropping. This is one reason why cancer patients are advised to take an easy walk after every meal—muscle movement helps drive the glucose to the muscles rather than cancer cells.

*Cancer Factor #9?*

Functional tests showed I had **gut dysbiosis**, an unhealthy collection of bacteria and/or fungi in the gut. It harms the immune system and increases cancer risk. Antacids, antibiotics, calcium supplements, elevated blood sugar, opioids, proton pump inhibitors, stress, and other factors contribute to dysbiosis.

Now researchers are looking at the microbiome in the mouth. They say you should not allow chlorinated water, fluoride, or any other antibacterial substance into your mouth because of the impact on the microbiome.

We must protect our microbiome to preserve our immune system, because it has the job of killing the cancer cells that we get on a routine basis. Yes, EVERYONE gets cancer cells, and your amazing immune system will kill them—if you're healthy.

The human body has spent thousands of years adapting to the world biochemically. It makes sense that our bodies cannot handle all the modern-day assaults on our biochemistry and microbiome. Research suggests it's best to do what was done for thousands of years—eat unprocessed whole foods, farmed the old-fashioned way, processed the way they were before the days of electricity and refrigeration. That includes soaking, sprouting, and fermentation. These processes help reduce irritating anti-nutrients and increase nutrient load. Other foods might include organic, pastured livestock, wild animals, or wild-caught seafood, but what's best for you depends on your goals. No matter what, we need to respect these ancient biochemical processes.

*Cancer Factor #10?*

I was significantly contaminated with **toxic chemicals** such as:
- heavy metals—mercury, lead, cadmium, arsenic, thallium etc.
- a chemical found in gasoline fumes called MTBE
- polystyrene used in containers for carryout food, eggs, etc.
- perchlorate from bleach, city water, and some organic veggies
- the herbicide 2,4-D found in Agent Orange and lawn chemicals
- glyphosate, the herbicide used on agricultural crops

For glyphosate, I was at the 95th percentile among humans tested for contamination, even though I had never worked with herbicides! However, after two years of eating organic food, I'm now at the lowest level they can detect. I'm almost there!

Unfortunately, organic food might also pose problems. For example, organic farmers spray copper sulfate on apples, grapes, tomatoes, and potatoes to control fungus. Some sources say it's also carcinogenic. I don't know but I have a chart showing extra high copper levels in various types of cancer, whatever that means. Other substances permitted in organic farming may also prove to be hazardous. And we've learned that organic fields might contain heavy metals, which are also carcinogenic. The "organic" label gives us no assurance that the food—or the coffee, tea, and cocoa you drink—is free of these. I'm always searching for food and beverage companies that test their organic products for heavy metals.

I know this can be discouraging, but taking action is a great antidepressant. We can decide what we purchase or refuse to purchase, when to call elected officials, and which politicians should be fired. In the meantime, I control what I CAN control, and I don't stress about the rest.

*Cancer Factor #11?*

Speaking of toxins, we must consider my consumption of **alcohol**. Remember when I said I had been hanging out with wine drinkers? That timing would be about right, although no one can say exactly when the cancer started.

*Cancer Factor #12?*

Let's add **mycotoxins**. One type comes from a Fusarium mold that can grow in homes. At about the time my cancer may have started, I was living in an apartment that had a moldy smell. I later discovered water standing in the air vents in the concrete slab floor. Another carcinogenic mycotoxin is aflatoxin B from Aspergillus mold, sometimes found in corn, other grains, nuts, and other foods.

*Cancer Factor #13?*

I know this is controversial, but I think **CT scans** are a danger and should be investigated by people with no conflicts of interest.

We know the ionizing radiation of X-rays causes DNA damage, along with various drugs, other toxins, gut bacteria problems, parasites, sunlight, etc. We all get a certain amount of radiation from sunlight and our environment known as "background radiation." The AMOUNT of radiation we receive, either all at once, or cumulatively over our lifespan, is the risk factor. The human body can repair DNA to some extent, but that is perhaps one of the causes of cancer—when the body no longer can keep up with the repair needed for whatever reason.

The amount of radiation in a CT scan can average 70—250 times that of an ordinary X-ray.

When I was in my 30s I had a mysterious abdominal pain that was never diagnosed. Probably stress. During that time I got two abdominal CT scans to try to identify the cause of my pain. In terms of radiation, ONE abdominal CT scan is equivalent to getting 2.7–6.6 years' worth of background radiation all at once. The amount mostly varies according to how the clinician sets the technical parameters on the scanner. The person's body size should be considered—some machines weigh your body and adjust the radiation dose, but I don't know if ALL machines do that, or if they made that adjustment for me more than thirty years ago at that particular location.

Oncologist #1 in Cancer State #1 tried to pooh-pooh my concerns about the previous two CT scans. I responded, "Oh. Well, all I know is, when I got the second one, the tech actually said to me, 'Are you sure you want to do this? This is a lot of radiation!'"

He just gave me an annoyed look. I did not mention this to him, but I also remembered the opinion of an emergency room doctor, younger than Onc #1, and from a more health-conscious state. My daughter had been in a car accident and had bumped her head. I asked if they were checking for a brain bleed using CT scan, because a famous actress had just died from a head injury that caused an undetected brain bleed.

The doctor responded, "Because she's still young, we don't want to give her a CT scan because we have no way to predict how many others she might need later in life. We want to watch how much total radiation people are exposed to. Instead we'll have her roommate wake her every two hours to make sure her brain is functioning." If the roommate discovered a problem, the doctor believed a prompt trip to the ER would be sufficient to handle the emergency.

A dental hygienist alerted me to the fact that the American Dental Association has changed its recommendation for dental X-rays, specifically to reduce radiation exposure. The ADA acknowledges in its *Journal* guidelines, "Ionizing radiation is a known carcinogen." From what I could see in a brief look at the guidelines, X-ray intervals are now 18–36 months or more, depending on the individual patient's tendency toward decay or infection.

Although the newer digital imaging exposes patients to less radiation, we patients would have to ask providers what kind of equipment they have. Beyond that, an article published through the National Institutes of Health shows why we should be careful about believing simplistic reassurances from providers. Take a look at what they say regarding digital imaging being safer:

> "It was once thought that digital systems would reduce radiation doses. They can facilitate dose monitoring by recording factors that have direct bearing on radiation exposure to patients, such as x ray tube voltage and tube current. Any technical errors can be promptly rectified, thus further reducing risk to the patient. Although some studies have shown dose reductions, there is a tendency towards increased doses. The reasons include the fact that

overexposure can go undetected, unlike with film, where the image turns dark, but more important factors are a tendency to take more images than necessary and at a higher image quality (and hence radiation dose) than necessary."[37]

**The FULL TRUTH in any science discussion is more complicated than some providers would have us believe. As that article shows, the devil is in the details.**

My concerns about dental X-rays and fluoride were relayed to a retired dentist who didn't know I'd be seeing his response. He defended digital imaging as perfectly safe. He showed no awareness of the other concerns described in this NIH article. In fact, he made a statement that proved the NIH correct! He said that, because he thinks digital imaging is so safe, he has chosen to X-ray some patients MORE than once per year. That is one of the points the article is making—that when imaging is believed to be safe, providers take more images, which partly defeats the purpose of using the safer technology! Plus let's remember the NIH article pointed to additional dangers.

Regarding fluoride, he referred to people who have concerns as "idiots." If I were speaking to him, I'd suggest he look at research about the effect of fluoride on the mouth microbiome, the thyroid, and other body systems. Then I'd be tempted to hand him this book, because his response leads us back to the very first points I made—**the need for HUMILITY and RESPECT**. That's especially true in the field of science. Good scientists hesitate to speak with certainty, and as cancer researcher and author Dr. William Li has said, "They talk more about what they DON'T KNOW."

**That dentist's attitude is one thing this book is campaigning against: Aren't we all DONE with condescending attitudes,**

**especially in the field of medicine? Here's that refrain: "No! We're not putting up with this anymore!"**

I believe MRI technology is advancing, and I wonder if it could eventually replace all CT scans. I know that MRI technology is already superior for some purposes, especially when using diffused weighted imaging (DWI). But beware: Not all DWI is created equal. I learned that the hard way. Some institutions do not have top-of-the-line equipment and software. But elsewhere, I have done a side-by-side comparison of whole-body DWI MRI and CT scan: It appears that high-quality DWI MRI is just as good examining even a body part where CT scan is supposed to be superior—the lungs. I've also read that the skill and experience level of the radiologist is especially important with MRI.

I now insist on MRI, but I refuse to use the MRI contrast agent gadolinium, because I read it collects in the brain and they're searching for a safer alternative. My experience tells me that if I can get to a top-quality DWI MRI facility, I don't need gadolinium anyway. But of course, I'm not dealing with all possible medical conditions—just my situation.

When I finally put my foot down and refused more CT scans, Onc #4 reminded me they're part of her standard process and she knows how to read them, but she agreed to my request for DWI MRI with no gadolinium. And recently we realized my blood tests are so accurate that we can probably dispense with imaging completely.

It's not easy making the medical establishment work in what you consider to be YOUR best interest. But if you value your health and your life, you'll analyze each situation for yourself.

**UPDATE:** Book writing/editing has taken more than a year. That's why I offer occasional updates—I'm always learning. I purposely left this section as is to demonstrate the uncertainty we all must experience as we raise concerns and search for truth. Not only must we endure our own self-doubt and fear of looking foolish, but also we might need to endure ridicule from others.

**Here's our call to courage: Science can't advance, and we can't be who we're meant to be, if we bend to those fears and pressures.**

So that said, here's a 2012 PubMed study I just "happened to find" today, when I wasn't even looking. It says ionizing radiation helps convert cancer cells to CANCER STEM CELLS. Cancer stem cells are cells that might START cancer, and also are well known for being resistant to both chemotherapy and radiation treatment. Thus, cancer stem cells help drive both recurrence and metastasis, which means spreading to other body parts. In other words, they are persistent agents of death. But what is happening in every town in this country that offers cancer treatment? Doctors ordering more and more CT scans. I don't know about you, but I've seen enough: "Ionizing Radiation Induces Stemness In Cancer Cells," on PubMed.[38] Also see endnote #39 for evidence of cancer risk resulting from CT scans.[39]

### *Cancer Factor #14?*

Remember my genetic problem (common to many of us) converting beta carotene to usable vitamin A? I have a second genetic mutation (common to perhaps 40% of us) that is associated with difficulties in detoxing and higher rates of cancer. This mutation, called **MTHFR C677T variant**, affects my ability to metabolize folate—vitamin B9. I am likely to have a 1/3 reduction in folate and an inability to convert the synthetic folic acid to folate. So I now know to consume folate-rich foods, take a high-quality folate supplement, and avoid that synthetic folic acid—as with beta carotene, there's a potential for toxic build-up because my body can't process it well.

Many of you have heard of that synthetic folic acid in prenatal vitamins because pregnant women take either folic acid or folate to prevent neural tube defects in their babies. One example of a neural tube defect is spina bifida—a spinal problem that causes numbness or paralysis in the lower extremities, plus other potential symptoms. I have a minor version called spina bifida occulta, which means it's not noticeable. This suggests my mother did not consume enough folate. I assume I inherited the genetic problem from her.

Way back when I was in college, at my first gynecological exam, they detected my double cervix and recommended an X-ray to check for duplicate kidney tubes, because of an association between the two problems. My kidneys were fine, but that's how a radiologist spotted the spina bifida occulta. But did I hear about it? No! I was told NOTHING until I went to deliver my first child a few years later. They told me I had spina bifida occulta and therefore could not receive an epidural. I had planned on natural childbirth, so it wasn't a big deal. But I sure would have appreciated knowing about my spinal condition when it was detected.

More importantly, someone should have explained to me my need for extra folate. From what I've read, at least by the time I was giving birth, scientists had already observed the connection between spina bifida and folate deficiency. The genetic test was not available until 2011, but I could have spent decades increasing my folate consumption, thereby helping my body detox and avoid cancer. Instead, I only learned of the folate problem 47 YEARS after that X-ray, and ten years after the test became available—only because a functional doctor was wise enough to test me.

Similar to the beta carotene example, I suggest we don't have to run everyone though genetic tests—maybe we just have to tell people how to eat to play it safe. In this case, if about 40% of us have this mutation, then it couldn't hurt to have everyone maximize folate consumption. Here's another example of how we're not given proper warnings, even though the knowledge is available.

*Cancer Factor #15?*

During the nine months prior to my stage-four cancer diagnosis, I took another supplement to try to help my eyes—**7-keto-DHEA**. I had read that DHEA is unsafe due to it hormonal nature but 7-keto-DHEA was safe. Now I wonder. More on that supplement in a bit.

# 19

## Cancer—State #1

After four months of continuous uterine bleeding, my chaotic life had settled down somewhat, so I finally called for a gynecological appointment. The woman offered a date a month away, so I said, "Okay, but I'll be checking around town for a different option because I don't want to wait that long."

She then said, "We have a cancellation for a week from today." Interesting how that opening suddenly entered her awareness, but yes, I would take that one.

At that first appointment I explained my use of HRT and how the bleeding started when I dropped the hormones. The doctor did not know what to make of that, but he asked me what else I'd been taking. I listed a few supplements but forgot about 7-keto-DHEA. That night, I realized I had forgotten to mention it, and I recalled reading it had a hormone-like effect, so I stopped taking it. My bleeding began to taper off, and by the third day, all bleeding was done. But then it felt like my uterus was swelling and abdominal pressure was increasing. I've never found a doctor who had an explanation for any of that.

After that, it was just a matter of days and I had the diagnosis— serous carcinoma of the uterus. The literature gave pessimistic predictions. This was not the more typical endometrioid uterine cancer that offers a better prognosis.

Although there are several types of uterine cancer, the literature I saw at the time identified two types. Type I was the endometrioid type and was estrogen positive. Type II included serous and others, and tended NOT to be estrogen positive. So based on those generalizations, because no one bothered to test my tumor, I assumed for over a year that my cancer was not estrogen positive. More recently, I've seen research stating that about 60% of Type II cases examined actually WERE estrogen positive! Identifying a cancer as estrogen positive is critical information. There are drugs and natural phytochemicals in food that block estrogen.

But with uterine cancer, the traditional protocol is limited to pharmaceuticals tested on a whole herd of diverse patients. For my cancer, they just rule out certain genetic issues, and they test for HER2 positivity.

HER2 positive tumor cells have a significant number of HER2 protein receptors. The "HER2" stands for human epidermal growth factor receptor 2, a receptor that drives the cancer to be more aggressive, making survival chances even worse. I tested highly HER2 positive, but that was good news, they said, because they had a monoclonal antibody called trastuzumab (brand name Herceptin) that would disrupt the HER2 signaling.

The only problem was that other cells, such as heart cells, also have HER2 receptors, so there was risk of heart damage. But not to fear! The initial research suggested the heart damage would not be permanent, and besides, not everyone experiences the damage anyway. (Remember that for later.)

One of the realities of the cancer world is that you are often asked to choose between two evils, and take YOUR BEST GUESS as to which will be the lesser evil. Will the cancer drug be worth the damage you incur? No one gives you guarantees. I have had four different oncologists in four different states. I have lost count of how many times one of them has answered a question with, "We don't know. We just don't have the data."

Finally, to Onc #4 (my favorite, by the way), I said, "Well, then how do you all practice medicine? How do you make decisions?"

She had no answer, but I've heard from experts that all traditional doctors follow the standard, overgeneralized protocols called "standard of care." There was one bright, beautiful exception, and you'll hear about it later.

In this book I'm sparing you almost all the technical details, because I'm covering many aspects of life from a holistic perspective. I don't think I should get into the biochemical weeds. That might bore some people and scare others, and I don't want anyone to quit reading—**there's too much at stake for your survival!** However, just this once, I want to show you my handwritten notes about trastuzumab:

> With trastuzumab, oxidative stress occurs and helps to cause heart damage. The drug inhibits ErbB2-ErbB4. The damage **MAY** be due to inhibition of neuregulin-1 activated pathway **OR** mitochondrial dysfunction due to altered BCL-XL/BCL-XS, which **LIKELY** leads to loss of mitochondrial membrane integrity resulting in loss of electron transport generation of free radicals, uncoupling of oxidative phosphorylation, which leads to ATP

reduction, release of pro-apoptotic proteins such as cytochrome C.

THAT is what I call getting into the biochemical weeds! One important takeaway is that even the medical community and pharmaceutical industry often do not fully understand the drugs they are using. Notice the words I put in bold, which reveal uncertainty. They're not sure HOW the drug causes heart damage. But I don't want you to rely on my notes. Here's a citation:

> "Unfortunately, the mechanism involved in causing the cardiotoxicity is still not completely understood." ("Mechanisms and potential interventions associated with the cardiotoxicity of ErbB2-targeted drugs," *Cellular and Molecular Life Sciences,* April 2020).

It has been quite common for me to see uncertainty in the research. I can understand uncertainty as scientists are learning new things, but I think the uncertainty is a problem when the medical establishment is PUSHING a drug without fully understanding the risks to the patient, or worse, HIDING the risks. I believe this is an issue not just in the cancer world, but in the entire medical industry, and I bet you can name some examples.

Believe it or not, I've even seen researchers write they are uncertain as to why a drug WORKS! *If you don't understand WHY a drug works at that biochemical level of detail, how can you know if you're causing some kind of downstream biochemical damage?*

Clinical trials are supposed to catch problems, but I've seen more than once that problems might not be discovered or admitted to for years. I realize that, in some cases, people are dying, so there's a rush to get drugs out there to try to help. Where the problem becomes morally reprehensible, though, is when the uncertainty or even the known risks are HIDDEN from patients, or the older, safer, less expensive solutions are hidden or publicly maligned.

Yes, of course, cancer patients are given a basic list of possible side effects of each drug, and the list states which symptoms warrant calling the doctor. But in my experience, those lists are incomplete, and I've seen doctors who don't care if you report a side effect from the call-your-doctor list. The issue is minimized or ignored.

**I think patients should know all the information from both research AND clinical experience, using a robust reporting system. I've asked countless times for answers based on actual clinical experience, and I've been told that such data does not exist. Wouldn't drug companies monitor clinical experience? If not, why not?**

Following the protocols established for broad categories of women, I would receive three cancer drugs. The monoclonal antibody, trastuzumab/Herceptin, had first been approved 23 years earlier. Paclitaxel had been approved 29 years earlier, and carboplatin had been approved 32 years earlier.

These last two drugs were traditional chemotherapy drugs, meaning they indiscriminately kill ALL fast-dividing cells. As you may know, rapid cell replication occurs in the hair follicles, the gut lining, the inside of the mouth, and the bone marrow—where blood cells and immune cells are created. That's why cancer patients might lose hair, suffer gut issues, have mouth sores, and suffer reduced immunity from damaged bone marrow. It looks like I still have gut damage from chemotherapy, with a reduced ability to absorb nutrients from food, which I know only because of functional tests.

How do I fight off future cancer if I can't maximize my basic health?

These chemotherapies are supposed to help because MOST cancer cells divide rapidly, so chemotherapy should kill them. But I was never told CANCER STEM CELLS don't divide that much. So chemotherapy, generally speaking, does not kill them. Also, these cells are REALLY GOOD at pumping out toxins and defending themselves, and they're resistant to radiation treatment. There might be other cancer cells lying dormant, so chemo might also fail to kill them.

I gradually learned all this from functional sources, who also criticize the whole "killing" approach, because as usual it does nothing to eliminate root cause. Let's say hypothetically you COULD kill all cancer cells everywhere in your body. What's to stop you from creating more when the root cause is never eliminated?

WHY ARE ROOT CAUSES IGNORED BY TRADITIONAL ONCOLOGY?

One hope is that your immune system can recognize and kill a few cancer cells in the future, once that bigger tumor burden is removed. And I hope that can happen. But that assumes your immune system can return to functioning normally. Strictly speaking, if your immune system had been functioning normally, you wouldn't have had a cancer diagnosis in the first place! And I just explained that chemo itself can damage the immune system. So one of the ugly ironies is that the drug used to kill cancer might make it harder for your natural immune system to kill cancer in the future!

Sigh. Well, back when I knew less and I was agonizing over whether or not to have chemo, I at least knew I wanted a hysterectomy. I wanted that malformed cancerous uterus OUT. I knew the cancer could be metastasizing to other parts of my body at any time.

But the local bureaucracy did not feel the same sense of urgency. I was informed that this huge institution in this major metropolitan area only had ONE surgery scheduler, and she was busy fighting with insurance companies to get authorization for all kinds of surgeries. I was under so much stress that now I don't recall how I learned about this, but I must've talked to some "angel" who worked there and gave me the inside scoop. The reason I know this NOW is I kept the letter that I wrote to my surgeon/oncologist, asking for accelerated scheduling. I outlined my situation:

- I had first sought medical care now more than a month earlier.
- I had mistakenly assumed my bleeding was due to dropping HRT, which led me to delay investigation.
- I mentioned the 7-keto-DHEA and the apparent acceleration in growth.
- I highlighted the news about the surgery scheduler.
- I told him honestly I was leaning toward avoiding chemo, so my chance of survival would be enhanced by earlier surgery.
- I said I'd heard HE had the power to expedite the surgery.

**Many people, including some medical personnel, have complimented me on how I have advocated for myself, saying that's what you HAVE TO DO in today's medical world. I agree. I'm sure I would not be alive today if I had not done so.**

I felt this request had to be a formal letter, delivered to the office. I believe I've learned, if you want to be taken seriously, you put things in writing, especially in a world driven by fear of liability. Lo and behold, my surgery was scheduled for one week away!

I went in with a positive we're-going-to-war attitude. My thought: No matter what procedure we're facing, once we have peace about moving forward, we go with enthusiasm! We're cheerful with medical staff and we express appreciation. They deserve that, and they tell me compliments are all too rare. Also, we should not hesitate to ask questions or speak up when we want a change.

So the surgery was done and healing went well. Two weeks later, I visited a different oncologist for a second opinion about whether or not to have chemo. I had not yet realized the pervasive pressure to stick with standard of care.

I'll give this second oncologist credit: In a moment of honesty, he said, "A hundred years from now, they're going to look back and call chemotherapy 'barbaric.'"

*Heck,* I thought, *I've known for decades that chemotherapy is barbaric. I've heard, "If the cancer doesn't kill you, the chemotherapy will." What's with this "hundred years"?*

I did not care for this doctor, so I kept searching for options. Despite my concerns about chemo, the holistic world was not offering solutions that earned my full confidence. Whatever I decided, I'd be betting my life. I had to FEEL right about each and every decision, given what I knew at that moment.

Those of us who believe in the Holy Spirit seek a special kind of guidance as we go along. Without that, I probably would have gone insane under the pressure, but that doesn't mean I'm well practiced in tuning into the Spirit. It's a learning process and a matter of faith development. So I did a massive amount of research, with help from one of my daughters. Having her as a partner was incredibly comforting! And I trusted the Holy Spirit to put the right research in front of our eyes. I also felt a kind of comfort because I sensed I was called to go through a learning process. **I always felt, deep in my spirit, that I was doing all that work not just for myself, but also for all of you.**

One of the first books I read was *How To Starve Cancer* by Jane McLelland, a woman in the United Kingdom who fought off stage-four cervical cancer in the 1990s by doing her own research, consulting multiple doctors, and using chemo, diet, exercise, supplements, and repurposed drugs to "starve" the cancer. See my website for more on those topics. Jane went back and forth between traditional oncology and a handful of functional doctors, and went through hell trying to get the answers she needed. Some doctors were kind and helpful, but others felt threatened by her ability to think for herself and ask intelligent questions.

Still, despite opposition she has called "traumatic," she persevered and became ONE OF THE VERY FEW IN HER SITUATION TO SURVIVE. She said the whole situation was so traumatic that, years later, she did not want to have to write a book. But thank God she did! **THERE WAS MY ROLE MODEL!** Without reading her book and seeing a brave role model, I probably would not be alive today. Thank you, Jane!

Roughly following Jane's example, I consulted a holistic cash-pay doctor and was placed on 15 supplements and seven repurposed drugs prescribed "off-label." Plus, he scheduled infusions into my bloodstream. He offered no opinion on whether I should also do chemo. He wouldn't take on that liability. I can't blame him.

The oncologist and holistic doctor did not communicate in any way, although they knew I was seeing both. Neither expressed concern about possible drug interactions. I decided I'd need to research. Pharmacists can check the pharmacy database for you, but I learned not all supplements are in their database. I also realized new information was being discovered all the time, so I couldn't bet my life that their database was up-to-date. As the days and months went by, I learned more and more about the side effects of all these substances in both oncology and holistic medicine. I also learned about possible interactions, plus harmful ingredients found in many supplements—the brand matters!

**This entire situation is why, as time passed, I became less and less compliant, less and less trusting, and I stopped various treatments as I learned more.**

The holistic doctor and a holistic pharmacist urged me to consult a holistic oncologist, so I delayed the chemo decision one week so that I could meet with him. To my dismay, he did not take me as a patient. Perhaps he did not want to be seen as stealing patients from other doctors. During that visit, I complained to him that the holistic literature said I could take all those supplements and drugs WHILE ALSO doing chemo, and that the supplements would help me survive with fewer chemo side effects. But the traditional side insisted those supplements would serve as antioxidants and undermine the effectiveness of the chemo!

"The holistic side says one thing, and the traditional side says the opposite. And I don't know who to believe, and I'm caught in the middle!" I wailed in desperation.

"Yes, you are," he said in a grave tone. He did his best to help by, first, suggesting a compromise—I should withhold the supplements, drugs, and infusions three days before chemo and three days afterwards. This was a more cautious approach compared to what the holistic doctor had recommended. He also sent me an article about the controversy.

More recently I followed traditional oncology's instructions and had only Turkey Tail mushroom powder, vitamin D3, magnesium, and turmeric spice or fresh root. But see my website about the risk of taking D3 without K2.

Although this holistic oncologist would not take me as a patient, he offered to run functional tests, and that's how I learned I was contaminated with glyphosate and other chemicals, and I'm extra bad at converting beta carotene. He advised me to lie to my oncologist and complain that the pre-med steroid called dexamethasone was causing me anxiety, so that Onc #1 would lower the dosage.

I refuse to lie, and I didn't want a battle. But fast forward to my most recent chemo, and I was able to persuade Onc #4 to cut the dosage twice, from 12 milligrams to eight, then four.

In that final week, I decided I should proceed with chemo and keep researching everything. I had to go day by day, researching enough to be ready for the next appointment. I was always under deadline with a major decision every couple of days, because some of the holistic treatments were three times per week. I could go to the appointment one day, but would I find research telling me to cancel the next appointment? That was the uncertainty I lived with for months.

But I wouldn't say that's all bad. It's a spiritual growth opportunity to understand we don't have all the answers, and the stakes are incredibly high, but we're going to walk by faith, just doing the best we can. WE HAVE TO LEARN TO TRUST if we're going to avoid a nervous breakdown! So even this nightmare was an opportunity for personal growth.

The chemo plan was to receive paclitaxel first, followed by carboplatin, followed by trastuzumab/Herceptin. According to the Internet, paclitaxel had to come first, because if carboplatin went first, it would stop paclitaxel from working. However, my current oncologist says, according to HER training, paclitaxel goes first because the reverse order is more TOXIC to the patient. Regardless of the reason, please remember that order for later.

I was still struggling to find peace about moving forward with chemo. I now, three years later, have heard of more people, including a former chemotherapy nurse, who refused chemotherapy for their advanced cancer and came out just fine. Holistic and functional strategies do matter. But I didn't have as much knowledge back then. I had just read books. *Could I trust them? What about my specific case?*

But at some point, with any hard decision, we run out of time and have to choose. So I opted for traditional AND holistic. Like the surgery, my approach was going to war. And I trusted God it would all work out regardless of any challenge I would face.

Even before cancer, I knew I was called to write a book to help all of you. I just had no clue I'd be writing about cancer. So whenever something bad happened during this cancer journey, I just said to God, "Well, there's ANOTHER episode to include in my book!"

**Turning every bad event into an advantage of some kind is a pretty good strategy. I highly recommend it for saving your sanity. Always look for a blessing—it's there. Sometimes it takes years to see it.**

*Chemo Day #1*

From the functional side, I'd learned it was important to fast for chemo. Cancer cells love glucose, as you know. Unlike healthy cells, which can rely on and even benefit from ketones from the liver during a fast, cancer cells might not have the same level of adaptability. Cancer types vary, but they tend to need glucose and the amino acid glutamine for their fuel. So the idea is, when you go to chemo in a water-and-electrolytes-only fast, those cancer cells are already weakened, right when chemo comes rushing through like a Mack truck.

Some advised fasting 72 hours before the chemo enters your system and a whole day after. I feared losing weight, but some functional docs say you lose mostly water in the first day or two, not fat or muscle. Some sources thought 12–48 hours would be enough. I was at about 40 hours when I showed up for Chemo Day #1.

I was feeling the effects of the fast: I think my blood sugar was extra low because of all the supplements I had been taking in prior days, but I was also filled with adrenaline, so I was ready to go to war. My chemo nurse checked me in, escorted me to my easy chair, and drew blood. Let's say her name was Mary. In my spirit, I felt good about her from the beginning!

Mary told me that during chemo I could have whatever I wanted from the hospital cafeteria. Well, I was hungry, and we all love food, and we all love "free." But no thanks! I would stick with my fast. And I had brought my own filtered water in a glass bottle.

A little later, Mary came over with a concerned look: "Your blood sugar is 48! It has to be 70 to receive chemo!" She said I'd have to drink orange juice to raise my blood sugar.

*Oh, no! Traditional medicine is going to try to ruin my fast!*

From Jane's book, I was prepared for a struggle, and here was a major battle right away! But what could I do? *Sigh.* I accepted defeat. She brought me four ounces of orange juice in a little plastic cup with a peel-off lid. *Ugh. No one should drink out of plastic.* But I very slowly sipped the juice, trying to slow down the blood sugar spike.

Mary stood there and watched me. I smiled at her and said, "I'm sorry to be a pain, but we're the ones who survive!" Mary smiled back. She never said a word but in my spirit I knew she agreed.

Mary drew blood again. It was 87, but Mary must have had the clinical experience to wait for my insulin to kick in. (Poor Mary probably didn't know that insulin drives cancer growth—that's one reason why blood sugar spikes are devastating.) The next check, a half hour later, showed my blood sugar had plummeted to 44! It seems my pancreas and the residual supplements in my body were working well!

Mary stood there and gave me a look that said, "What are you going to do about this?"

I said, "Okay, go ahead and bring me some broccoli, green beans, and almonds." Someone made a run to the cafeteria and then I ate my food. Blood sugar now at 80, Mary was satisfied we could begin.

That night, I went home to research that rule that my blood sugar had to be 70 or above. In about three minutes, I found an article stating 70 only applied to diabetics! Non-diabetics like me could be down to 55! So I sent that article to my oncologist's nurse and said I'd be trying for 55 from now on. The doctor's office never admitted the hospital policy was wrong, but three weeks later at the next chemo, Mary showed me the written instructions she had received—allow the patient to be at 55 or above.

Whew! First battle won! But the effectiveness of Chemo Day #1 was probably reduced, along with protection from side effects. During those first three weeks, I experienced the numb fingers from neuropathy, fatigue and shortness of breath, one day of minor nasal bleeding, and achy muscles. No nausea or hair loss.

### Chemo Day #2

Early that morning, I broke my fast with sauerkraut and olives because I felt so weak. Mary's blood draw showed glucose above 70. She was pleased but I wasn't. Now I had a second day with a ruined fast, but my fault this time.

After the infusion of pre-meds I noticed a memory problem I'll explain later, but no other issues until the early morning hours of the fourth day—just about when, according to my calculations, the steroid would be out of my system. I woke up early that morning to loud tinnitus—a whining in my ears. It was maddening! I thought, *If I have to listen to this for the rest of my life, I'll go insane!*

As soon as the office opened, I made an urgent call to my oncologist's nurse navigator. Some standard drug sheets list potential hearing issues for both paclitaxel and carboplatin. I had also read one research study on carboplatin where a small percentage of people experienced hearing loss. The nurse navigator quickly called me back, but she tried to tell me that carboplatin does not produce hearing loss. "That's cisplatin," she said.

"No, cisplatin was 5.75% of the patients, and carboplatin was 3.5%!" For writing this book, I checked a meta-analysis summarizing many studies: Over 49% of patients had hearing loss with cisplatin and over 13% with carboplatin.

I told her I'd rush to have my hearing tested. Sure enough, I had a 5–20 decibel drop in hearing across all frequencies. I only know that because I had read that patients should have a baseline hearing test prior to the first cancer treatment. My doctor hadn't told me this—I had to ask for it. Unfortunately, I discovered that information a little late, so my first hearing test was squeezed in the day AFTER my first chemo. That's not an accurate baseline, but my second test proved the hearing loss was AT LEAST that bad, if not worse.

To add to my fun that week, my hair decided to drop out—all of it, instantly. We're warned to expect it, but that's never a happy day.

So the next question was, *what are we going to do to protect those ears?* I was told the next chemo would be delayed a week so we could figure that out. Spacing chemo further apart would reduce its effectiveness, but there was no other choice, as far as I knew. Through the nurse navigator, Onc #1 asked me if my HOLISTIC DOCTOR had any ideas! My holistic doctor had a few ideas for treatments in his office, but nothing that would protect me DURING chemo. So I had another research project ahead of me.

In my research, I found a drug called sodium thiosulfate. When I mentioned it to Onc #1, he did not seem familiar with it. I also suggested antioxidants such as melatonin that had been shown to offer ear protection. He seemed to push the decision onto me and said we'd talk later.

So I launched into another research frenzy. It seemed the decision was on my shoulders, believe it or not. That's why I was shocked when, in the next discussion, he was upset with me for selecting melatonin. It seemed he had wanted me to select sodium thiosulfate! Apparently, he had finally asked around and been told about the drug.

So we were going with sodium thiosulfate. Then I did MORE research to learn about this drug. I found a few worrisome facts, and I realized I would need to raise concerns at the next chemo. Remember that earlier, he had not expressed any familiarity and had asked if the holistic doctor had ideas. I thought this was a new experience for them, especially because he had defended his nurse navigator's ignorance, saying they had never seen hearing loss with carboplatin in the gynecological oncology department.

### Chemo Day #3 (Attempted)

When I finally showed up for Chemo Day #3, after a week's delay, you'd better believe I was in a deep fast. I knew that I had let up on my fast that second day, and I had been hit with hearing loss plus massive and sudden hair loss. Now that I had permission to have my glucose down to 55, I was more determined than ever. I hoped fasting could save my ears.

Each chemo day, I would now have a preliminary meeting with Onc #1, after the blood draw but before the results came back. We started our little meeting in a private room off the chemo area. The room was sparsely furnished. Onc #1 and I had chairs to sit on, facing one another, while the oncologist's nurse and nurse navigator had to stand nearby and watch the discussion. In each of those meetings, they always remained silent.

My first request was to reduce my Benadryl, another one of those pre-meds to reduce allergic reaction to chemo. From my research, I figured that had been the cause of my memory problem. All I know for sure is, on Chemo Day #2, I had trouble conversing with Mary. I would ask her a question or make a comment, but as I listened to her answer, I suddenly couldn't recall my own question or comment! And it happened multiple times! I thought, *Now I know what dementia must feel like!* When I asked about that, Onc #1 said he'd cut the dosage in half. I never had that problem again.

After that, we turned to discussing my fourth drug, the sodium thiosulfate. I took that opportunity to pull out my notes, and I tried to ask about the two different dosages, because I'd read the higher dosage could cause a brain seizure! With a wave of his hand he shut me down.

"You're getting too far into the weeds!" he charged. "And if you're going to read, you should read good material like PubMed!"

"I AM reading PubMed," I told him. He ignored that.

I leaned forward and continued, "I'd just like to get reassurance about this one thing—" He interrupted me to say they didn't need information, but I was asking for REASSURANCE more than offering information!

"Oh," I responded. "Well if you've never used sodium thiosulfate before, then I thought—"

He interrupted me again: "We HAVE used it before!"

I was confused at that point because he'd claimed they'd never had anyone with hearing loss before. But then I guessed his use of the word "we" must have meant the entire hospital, not just the gynecological oncology department. But I thought, *I am NOT going to have a brain seizure because I was intimidated into not sharing this last piece of information!*

So I leaned forward again to show him my notes and I persisted: "Okay, but I just want to show you that, in addition to discussing dosage, they're also talking about the infusion rate. If it goes in too fast, the patient can have a brain seizure."

*There! It was out!* He was absolutely disgusted with me, but I had gotten my information out there, and now they'd been warned and the liability was on them. I felt extremely relieved, like a terrible weight had fallen off my chest. I went on to explain cheerfully, "I thought no one here had used it before, but if the hospital has experience with it, then I'm sure everything will be fine!" I just kept smiling and looking right at him.

My sudden expression of cheerful confidence must have thrown him for a loop! The meeting was quickly terminated. That had not been fun, but I left feeling relieved that I had stood my ground and accomplished one of my goals for our communication. And I had explained what I had been thinking, which should have reduced his annoyance. He really had not communicated clearly with me, so I had to piece things together. That little episode had required persistence! But I was not going to take a chance on a brain seizure.

**Here's a key point for all your dealings with people: I could not control what THEY did, but I had taken responsibility and done MY part. I was learning how to do MY part and then relax and leave the rest to God.**

Back to my easy chair I went. A while later, good ol' Mary came over, pushing her little computer stand mounted on wheels. "They've just changed your infusion time for that drug," she said. "They've doubled the time from 30 to 60 minutes."

"Oh, that must be because I just warned them about the possibility of a brain seizure if they infuse it too fast."

I noticed amusement on her face, but she only said, "The pharmacist looked it up and a 60-minute infusion rate was also an option in his database." So that took care of that, I imagined.

A while after that, my labs came back, and Mary was concerned: My bilirubin had more than doubled from 0.6 on Chemo Day #2, to now above the acceptable range, sitting at 1.5. That was a sign of liver damage, she said.

*Hmmm.* I knew NOTHING about bilirubin, except newborns might have a temporary problem with it, and the natural solution was to let them sunbathe. But it suddenly came to me in a supernatural way:

"Maybe that's because of the difference in my fasting level," I suggested.

"No," she responded. "We don't think your level would have doubled just because of that."

*Hmmm.* Well, they knew more about it than I did, right? It was clear she had already consulted my oncologist, who had gone back to his office. So they sent me down via wheelchair ride to a lower floor for a sonogram of the liver, and then I was dismissed until my bilirubin could test within range. Chemo Day #3 was delayed another week.

That afternoon, I did a quick check on my computer. Sure enough, bilirubin levels can rise due to fasting, and one study showed they had doubled. I then looked at what my bilirubin had been on Chemo Day #1. That day, it was ALSO high, near the top of the range at 1.1. Because it was just within range, nobody noticed and nobody cared. But I saw the pattern: Day #1—pretty deep fast, and bilirubin was high at 1.1. It was measured from the INITIAL blood draw before that forced feeding. Then Day #2—I broke my fast, and my bilirubin was back down at 0.6. And then Day #3, the deepest fast of all, and bilirubin was the highest of the three at 1.5. My labs proved the Internet article correct.

So I sent ANOTHER email to my oncologist's nurse to explain the whole situation. She responded that, before I could have my third chemo, I'd need a good bilirubin test. So I was tested three days later. Of course there was no need for fasting that day, so my bilirubin was back down. No liver damage. But my chemo effectiveness had been once again diminished by another delay, all because they didn't know what they didn't know.

### *Chemo Day #3 (Actual)*

The REAL Chemo Day #3 finally came, and I was set to receive that fourth drug. That meant an extra long day—each drug required its own infusion time. Even when I had three drugs, I was the last to leave, somewhere around suppertime. Most people only had one or two drugs. Adding the fourth drug might keep me there until 9:30 p.m.

When I settled into my easy chair I asked my chemo nurse for a new printout to confirm the changes. I had a new nurse that day, a younger one. And good ol' Mary was sweet enough to come over and say I should not take it personally, but she'd been assigned to manage the floor, and that's why I had a different nurse. I really appreciated her telling me that, and of course I was fine with that. I'm a very agreeable and easygoing person, believe it or not! I just think, if my life's on the line, things should be the best we can make them, right?

After they'd collected my blood, I was called into the meeting room to talk with Onc #1. We went over our additions and dosage changes. And by then, Annoying Carol had another question. As you know, I was always moving just one day at a time. You never knew what I'd find in the research. Each time, I knew I was committing to one more chemo, but not necessarily to all six, as their protocol suggested.

I had now seen research out of Japan that, for uterine cancer, six treatments gave no better survival than four. The last two treatments—the fifth and sixth—only produced more side effects. And some of those could be permanent, like neuropathy so bad you couldn't button a shirt! So I asked about that question of four vs. six.

Oooh, that did it! Onc #1 started lecturing me on how he had been to four years of medical school, and I just had to trust him. He again attacked the idea of my reading and also the QUALITY of my reading: "You should be reading PubMed, not these…." I don't recall his exact description of bad sources of information.

I refrained from saying I'd already told him the week before—I just calmly repeated, "I AM reading PubMed."

He continued to attack my reading, and I know my stress hormones were up because I felt unfairly attacked—after all, it was MY LIFE we were talking about, and hadn't all our past experience together taught him that he and the hospital don't always know everything they SHOULD know? It's just too bad for them that the patient was discovering information that revealed their ignorance—ignorance that was jeopardizing my life!

Does anyone think I WANTED it to be that way? Who needs the stress of going up against a system, or the heartbreak of feeling so uncared for? Wouldn't a little bit of humility have been appropriate for him right then? And some intellectual curiosity? And a desire to learn and be ever-improving as a doctor? WHY COULDN'T WE WORK AS A TEAM?

Go ask business experts! They'll tell you about being on a growth path and harnessing the power of teamwork to create a better product or a more efficient process, and that includes customer input. Why was the medical world in the egotistical Stone Age with their bully's club and barked-out commands? *Just shut up and do as you're told! You have NOTHING to offer—just be a good little sheep and help us generate income for the system.*

I didn't expect him to know everything, and I had great respect for all that he DID know, and to this day, I think he did a fantastic job on my surgery. But why shoot me for trying to improve patient care? What was his top priority—the quality of my care and the care of future patients, or protecting his ego?

I ask these questions because we were coming off this recent debacle, canceling my chemo over nothing except raised bilirubin due to fasting. And they had probably hampered my first chemo by forcing me to eat, simply because they didn't know the rules for non-diabetics.

But at that moment, all my spiritual growth from so many years was with me—a strong sense of identity and alignment with God, countless examples of pushing myself to face interpersonal challenges, even a toughening from learning to stay calm and cheerful in the presence of abusers, and the benefit of years of counseling, and a confidence from knowing that I had ALWAYS behaved appropriately with this man and his nurses—calmly, politely, cheerfully, with never even a hint of annoyance—that strong confidence built from facing adversity over and over until I could get it right and conduct myself in a way that I respected.

All those years of heartache and tears, but FACING MY FEARS and turning to God for strength, were now paying off, and so I quietly and calmly and kindly said, "I'm trying to make the best decisions I can, and I need information to do that."

A second of silence, and then I finished with one bold moment of truth: "With the blood sugar and the bilirubin, it seems we're all just learning as we go, and that's okay."

The law of healthy boundaries and the law of personal responsibility say it's not my job to protect his ego and shield him from the truth. It would be morally wrong, in this case, to do so. He needed to learn some life lessons. People's lives are being forever altered by the quality of our healthcare, or lack thereof.

And the Holy Spirit never told me I needed to keep my mouth shut to save my life. If he had been a truly malevolent force, I would have been guided to handle the situation differently. **This is why no one can tell you exactly what to say or do in a given situation. You need to be walking in the Spirit!**

But I had stood my ground in a confident and respectful way. I wasn't going to back down. I wasn't going to apologize. I would not be intimidated!

The meeting was quickly adjourned. The two nurses had, as usual, stood there like sentinels, silently observing the whole thing. I glanced their way as I exited the room, but I was moving too quickly to see their expressions. I had no idea what they had been thinking:

1. Were they annoyed with me?
2. Were they filled with anxiety over the tension in the room, tension that only HE was creating? Were they thinking, "Don't get him in a bad mood! Then WE'LL have to put up with him!"
3. Or as women, as nurses—a profession that I hear has historically taken a lot of crap from arrogant doctors—were they standing there secretly thinking, "You go, girl. So proud of you!"

I will never know. I'd like to imagine option #3!

As I passed through the doorway, I realized my gut was hurting from emotional stress. That's not good when you're fighting cancer. When I got back to my chair, Mary was fiddling with the computer on the rolling stand, just to my right. I glanced her way and said something like, "My gut's hurting from the emotional stress. Doctor is aggravated with me because of the reading that I do."

Mary didn't say anything, but my very skilled antennae did not sense any condemnation from her. Just then, my nurse for the day handed me the printout I'd requested and walked away. There was the fourth drug and the reduction in Benadryl.

*But wait a second!* My eyes caught something—they had switched the order so that carboplatin would come first, BEFORE paclitaxel. At that moment, I only had a vague memory of reading about the correct order. So I flipped open my laptop, and the first search result was Drugs.com. I read that, yes indeed, the order mattered. Carboplatin going first would render paclitaxel ineffective!

"Oh, no!" I cried out involuntarily, still staring at my computer screen. "He's gonna HATE me!" He had just reamed me for reading too much, and here I was, doing more reading!

Mary was still there to my right, I realized. "Is Drugs.com not a legitimate source?" I wailed. I explained the issue to her. She quickly called Onc #1. He claimed that had been disproven. But here's what I've learned:
- Immediately after that day in 2021, I saw in the research a DIFFERENT concern had been disproven.
- Even with its October 2024 update, Drugs.com still insists paclitaxel "MUST" come before carboplatin, or it will be ineffective against cancer, and I've seen PubMed research that supports this.

- My current oncologist, Onc #4, believes the incorrect order creates more bone marrow damage, and my labs support that also—I had a greater drop in neutrophils, a type of white blood cell, but I returned to typical patterns once we restored the original order.

Later in the day, Mary explained the hospital strategy was to get me out the door faster now that four drugs were involved. Because we had to give carboplatin four hours to work before the sodium thiosulfate, they wanted carboplatin first so that four hours could start ticking away while I received other drugs in between. Without saying these words, she let me know THEY WERE JEOPARDIZING MY LIFE TO KEEP FROM PAYING NURSES OVERTIME.

She explained the proper thing to do was, at closing time, admit me into the hospital so that a floor nurse could finish my infusions in the proper order. I would then be dismissed and never spend the night in my room. I'm so glad she clued me in. Another one of those angels!

But that morning, I did not have all this information. So I had carboplatin first.

A little bit later, after Mary had gone to attend to the rest of the floor, I asked my chemo nurse about ANOTHER CHANGE I saw on my sheet. Gone was Herceptin as my third drug. "Kanjinti" was in its place. When I asked my nurse about it, she said, "Oh, that's just the generic version of Herceptin."

I later learned that was incorrect, but I can understand her confusion: The monoclonal antibody trastuzumab (brand name Herceptin) cannot have a generic version. A generic drug is an exact copy of a brand name drug, but I've read monoclonal antibodies can't be exactly duplicated. So the cheaper competitors like Kanjinti are considered part of the trastuzumab family but can only be called "biosimilar."

As you'll recall, Herceptin had been around for over 20 years—Kanjinti only two! Looking at a bit of research, I saw that Kanjinti had a different side effect profile overall and a higher rate of serious adverse events. Plus, I knew a longer span of clinical experience might be helpful in discovering dangers!

I was not happy with a bait and switch that seemed to be about saving money. I was not sure what to make of the higher rate of adverse events. But what was I going to do? I could have pushed for Herceptin, but I have a vague memory that they warned a request for drug change would delay my treatment, assuming it was approved at all. The younger chemo nurse told me the first sheet was incorrect: I had not had Herceptin the first two days. It had been Kanjinti all along, she claimed. I could have raised a big stink on the basis of deception, but I didn't see enough reason in the research to justify pushing the issue, so I let that go. We all must pick our battles.

So I got carboplatin first, which I have to assume rendered paclitaxel ineffective and did more bone marrow damage. Then later that day, I got the long-awaited sodium thiosulfate.

Remember they had changed the infusion time from 30 to 60 minutes? Well, maybe that was a good thing. During the infusion, I quickly began to feel lousy, and I told the nurses they had better bring me a vomit pan. I managed not to vomit, finished the drug, gathered my belongings, and headed out the door so they could go home, clutching the vomit pan to my chest. About 30 feet down the hall, I vomited. The next day, I told my oncologist's nurse, and as I recall, they upped the infusion time to 90 minutes. I wonder what would have happened if I had said nothing and we had started with 30. Sigh.

But despite that hellish day, one of the greatest things happened, thanks to my angel of the chemo ward. Near the end of the day, Mary came over to my easy chair, bent down close, and said, "You keep reading. And you keep asking questions!"

If you've had the life experience I've had, at times starved for understanding and moral support, then you realize how precious that encouragement is to me. I will forever treasure that moment. It helped soothe me in the days that followed, as I researched the day's controversial topics. **Sometimes you just have to hold onto whatever blessing you DID receive, and let that sustain you.**

### Chemo Day #4 and #5

Once I had confirmed that Onc #1 was wrong about the order of the drugs, I realized my life was in jeopardy and began to look for an escape. In a nearby state was a more "outside-the-box" cancer clinic, so I planned a visit. Anytime we reach out to a new clinic, we must complete numerous forms and send up-to-date medical records. But I finally managed a visit the Thursday before the next chemo, which was scheduled for Monday. Time was running out.

This clinic was shockingly disorganized, and good care did not seem likely. So that Friday morning, I sent a message to Onc #1 through their portal. I basically said what I had seen in the research, and "it was my understanding" that the proper way to care for me was to admit me to the hospital that evening so that we could deliver the drugs in the correct order. I received a response that same day that they'd be willing to admit me and put the drugs back into the original order.

So Chemo Days #4 and #5 were uneventful. During that time, however, I might have given Onc #1 the impression that I was considering skipping #6 because of the research out of Japan recommending only four. I had split the difference and done five. I then received a very upsetting phone call from him.

Maybe he was trying to scare me into doing #6. All I know for sure is, he was "speaking death over me," as I call it. It was so upsetting I can't recall details.

Immediately after, I was on the phone sobbing loudly to my friend. I was outraged. She has always admitted to being more of a fearful pessimist, so she may have thought I was upset because I was hearing upsetting TRUTH. But if so, she didn't get it at all—she didn't understand how my mind and spirit work! I was upset because I deeply believed he was NOT speaking truth to me, that he did NOT have valid scientific reasons and moral justification for making those statements, and was therefore behaving wrongly and unprofessionally. I was experiencing a pro-death spiritual attack, because even if he had some statistical evidence on his side, he still had no business saying that. I think it's fine if a doctor feels it's time to suggest it "MIGHT BE" a good time to get personal affairs in order just in case, but that's different from predicting death!

I speak with confidence because we know about the power of the human mind: There are so many accounts of critically ill people who believed the negative statements of doctors and then rolled over and died, or just gave up on their own, while other patients shouted "No!" figuratively speaking, if not literally, and went on to prove those doctors wrong!

This negative fear mongering is SUCH a common problem in traditional medicine! Sometimes it's not a life-or-death issue at all—sometimes doctors are pressuring patients to take a drug, even though there is a cheaper, safer, healthier, more natural solution. I should probably mention that I've read at least some oncologists get a percentage cut of chemo profit, and doctors in general might get rewards for the prescriptions they write.

If Onc #1 had been sincerely looking out for my welfare, he would have respected my search for truth all along! He would have put my needs ahead of hospital profit. He would have taken a stand on principle with the hospital if necessary, even if it made his professional life difficult. But he didn't do ANY of that and I had to USE MY KNOWLEDGE TO PUT THE PRESSURE ON.

**You have to find the knowledge you need and use your power! I don't want you victimized!**

So I never did the sixth treatment. As usual, I took the full time to research, pray, and ponder, and then I let them know I wouldn't be coming. My friend had invited me to come to her state and stay with her while getting settled with new doctors. I had decided to do it.

Early the next morning, I got a call from the nurse navigator, who urged me to have another phone call with Onc #1. I told her I didn't see the point in that, because we really didn't have much to discuss. And why should taxpayers pay for that appointment, I would add now.

Believe it or not, she then said something about a need to discuss "end-of-life care." I paused on the phone. "DID YOU SAY END-OF-LIFE CARE?"

I have no idea whether she made a terrible mistake and the wrong phrase slipped out of her mouth, or she was being manipulative, or a spiritual force had taken over her mouth. But I wasn't having it. She tried to say she had meant a termination-of-service discussion. *Okay. Interesting Freudian slip, considering the nasty conversation I had with the doctor!* I repeated there was no need for discussion, and that was the end of that.

# 20
# Cancer—State #2

We can now move more quickly, but not because things went better!

At first I liked my new oncologist, Onc #2. I told her that, because of the new revelations about heart damage, I did not want to do maintenance doses of any drug in the trastuzumab family. The research I had recently found basically said, "Oops! The heart damage isn't temporary after all, and it can show up 3-5 years AFTER the drug is discontinued!"

She seemed to respect my concern, so I only saw her for the occasional check-up. But several months later, I got my first "positive" from a high-tech, circulating tumor DNA blood test that looked for my original tumor DNA. I'd had three negatives in a row, but now I had a positive. It was back, assuming it had ever left—I've already explained the difficulty in knowing whether chemo works, and you know how butchered my treatment was in State #1. So I allowed another CT scan, which showed "innumerable" nodules in my lungs.

But they said that could be an infection. So I was instructed to SIT AND DO NOTHING FOR TWO MONTHS, and then see if they've grown.

I'd already received the positive circulating tumor DNA test (ctDNA). But here's the problem: Although traditional oncology has had some amazing achievements, the field is also known for being strangely resistant to change for many cancer types. In MY experience in four states, the traditional oncologist won't offer the ctDNA test and has never even heard of it! I got started on it through one of the great cash-pay doctors that I consulted—let's call him Dr. Cutting Edge. The test is now so validated that Medicare covers it! But Onc #2 said the test was irrelevant.

Two months later, the next CT scan showed the nodules had grown. And now you and I know about research showing harm from CT scans.

Based on my reading, I'd say it's likely that cancer cells were in my lungs even before my surgery, or that cancer cells were scattered into the bloodstream DURING surgery. I hear more and more breast cancer patients are refusing a biopsy for this reason. They say, "Don't go cutting into the tumor and spilling its contents into my bloodstream. Just take the tumor out carefully." That's something to research if you're facing cancer.

Once they saw the nodules had grown, they were finally ready to discuss treatment. And they were recommending the next step in the standard protocol—immunotherapy called Keytruda. And because my histology did not suggest that Keytruda would be all that effective, the protocol called for a second drug called Lenvima, which they said would probably give me high blood pressure. They were also finally willing to test my tumor for estrogen positivity. The test said 20% estrogen positive.

"That's not much," Onc #2 told me, "No point in trying estrogen therapy. Now, if you were 90% that would be different."

*Rats! That estrogen therapy is WAY less toxic than immunotherapy.* But no, she said.

I wanted to see if anyone else had any bright ideas. I thought, *I'll get a second opinion at one of the most prestigious cancer research places in the U.S. They'll have something more cutting-edge!*

Nope, it was a waste of time and money, except for gaining a new analysis of my tumor histology and experiencing more trauma.

Enter Dr. Nazi #2. Remember I promised there would be a second one? Here she is. In the examination room, as she and her medical student were discussing my case, I made the mistake—I think—of mentioning that my mother had been given DES prior to my conception. I will always believe that's what led to the next event. She told me they'd need to do a gynecological exam. No one else I consulted had needed that, but I just figured this was a big research place, *so okay.*

The doctor stood by my head, while the student did the exam. As you may know, when you're flat on your back, you can't see what they're doing. Suddenly, I heard *kachoop, kachoop, kachoop*! And I felt pain at the back of the vagina.

"Ow!" I cried out. I craned my neck to look up at the doctor on my right. "Are you taking a tissue sample?" I asked in alarm. I thought they needed legal permission for that.

"No," she said.

"Well, that hurt!" I said.

"You can get dressed now," she said. "We'll meet you in my office across the hall."

I think I was too surprised, too used to abusers, and also too set on solving cancer to confront the doctor. My mind was just so focused—I knew "in my bones" that there was a way to survive, and I just had to find it. So I never brought up that shocking experience. Instead, we talked more about my case, with the medical student sitting next to her—looking very scared, I noticed.

Dr. Nazi #2 laid my pathology report on the desk. "You just aren't the typical serous," she said.

Rather than having the presence of mind to ask, "Why not?" I enthusiastically jumped into telling her one of my theories—that I wasn't really serous, because I had read when endometrioid progresses FAR ENOUGH, it starts to look like serous, and the pathologist can be fooled.

She had not heard of that research but glanced at my report. "No, given who signed your pathology report, I think you can trust the diagnosis."

She then proceeded to speak death over me. My attitude was, *Lady, you aren't talking about ME, so let's just move on to the next subject.* I suppose it looked to them like I had not heard her, but I had. I just wasn't having it.

That's the attitude we need to take when anyone tries to speak ANY doom and gloom over us, generally speaking. There will be times when we DO need to listen to a warning. But is it a warning that gives you a possible solution, even if it's a Hail-Mary pass? Or is it just pure hopelessness? There's the difference, and I think that tells you the SPIRITUAL SOURCE of the message, if you know what I mean.

Dr. Nazi #2 had only one suggestion—stick with immunotherapy. *Crap!* I didn't feel good about this. So back to my friend's I went.

But on the road, I had time to think about that painful exam. *What WAS that?*

Then out of nowhere, the phrase "punch biopsy" came into my head—not an audible voice but supernatural. I had heard of punch biopsy in dermatology, checking for skin cancer. But I'd never heard of it in gynecology, so I did some checking. Sure enough, punch biopsy could be done. And what was one of the few reasons WHY it would be done? To see if the patient had been exposed to DES!

Maybe there was my answer: Dr. Nazi #2 wanted some of my tissue to test for DES exposure for their research, and she wasn't about to ask my permission and risk being told no, which I would have done, because I knew that injuring me made me more prone to cancer spread. Cancer loves to go where there are wounds and other kinds of inflamed tissue. For weeks after that, I had cramping and pain from what I now believe was a punch biopsy. I confirmed the sound of the device with someone familiar with it.

When I saw Onc #2 a week later, I told her what had happened and asked her to check for a wound. Of course, after a whole week, perhaps she would not have been able to see anything. She said she didn't. She gave me this deer-in-the-headlights look. It was obvious she did not want to comment on what had happened. She acted like she knew no one at that institution, even though she had been in research earlier in her career. She also had claimed previously that oncologists have no way to communicate with one another and share their clinical experience—that was her defense for why they never had answers to my questions about actual clinical experience with various drugs. But several months later, she must have forgotten we had discussed that, because she let it slip that she was recently talking to someone from that same institution at a conference!

*Oh, I thought they never got together and communicated with one another, and yet she attends a conference? And I thought she knew no one at that institution, but it turns out she has had a long-term relationship with someone there? No wonder she gave me that deer-in-the-headlights look!*

I later told my new integrative GP about the punch biopsy. She had a pure heart, honesty, and a sense of right and wrong. Her instant response was, "That would be illegal!"

But there was nothing to be done. Another case of being violated. *Oh, well, add it to the long list and forget about it. I have cancer to survive.*

I asked my GP if she knew where I could find a more INTEGRATIVE oncologist there in State #2. Here was her honest response: "GET OUT OF STATE #2!"

Oooh, that wasn't a good sign. But I was here, at least for now, so I shook that off. But something Dr. Nazi #2 said kept running through my mind: "You just aren't the typical serous."

I messaged her through the portal, asking her what she had meant. No response. I called and posed my question to the staff. Dr. Nazi #2 responded through the portal—it was my estrogen positivity. Well, I already KNEW I was estrogen-positive, but only 20% according to the lab Onc #2 used. I had the newer histology analysis in my possession, and I didn't see anything earth-shattering. *Oh well.* I tucked it into my bin with stacks and stacks of other notes and medical records. I was accumulating quite a mess of paperwork.

So I started immunotherapy, and my abdominal discomfort grew worse and worse. What was causing it? I had never felt right since that punch biopsy. Did I have an infection? Was my discomfort due to advancing cancer? Or was it from the drugs? The drug sheets revealed the drugs could cause all kinds of abdominal pain. Onc #2 did not seem interested in finding out.

One night, as I was looking through my massive pile of papers for notes I could get rid of, I pulled out the histology report from that research institution. *Should I pitch this?* I wondered. *Well, if you're going to pitch it, at least read it carefully first to see if there's anything worth keeping.*

So I read it again—VERY CAREFULLY. And there, in the middle of page three, was a line that somehow my eyes had missed: MY ESTROGEN POSITIVITY WAS 90%! No wonder Dr. Nazi #2 was so taken by my estrogen positivity!

*Oh, my God!* All this time, here in State #2, I'd been told there was no benefit in hormone therapy because I was only 20% estrogen positive, and here was probably a more authoritative analysis saying 90%. That was the number that Onc #2 said would make a difference! And I've since heard you don't have to be up near 90 for a treatment to be effective.

I just about went through the roof with outrage: What kind of medical world are we dealing with, where two tests have such different results? And then a drastically more expensive treatment is justified on the basis of those results, which could be wrong? Is no one noticing these discrepancies in the industry? Does anyone care about test reliability and validity and doing the best for the patient?

It's not a legitimate explanation to say a tumor is a mass of different kinds of tumor cells—which it actually can be—and one lab happened to get one little piece, and a different lab a different piece. For diagnosis, you'd need enough of a sample for the test to help you attack the whole tumor! Who is checking this industry for quality control?

And do you realize: Test inaccuracy is probably seldom discovered by patients and doctors because most cancer patients NEVER GET MORE THAN ONE TEST and most doctors would never order the test from more than one company! Only people like me talk to multiple doctors around the country and end up getting multiples tests. And that was just a by-product of my consulting different doctors. I had no idea they'd advocate for a test done by a different company. I had not previously known these tests even existed. I have innocently stumbled upon this information, and I wish it weren't true!

And get this—with a different doctor, who used a different company, I have a third report that says 50%. Was the research institution the correct analysis, coming in at 90? I think so, because I later had ascites fluid from my abdomen analyzed by a hospital pathologist and those cancer cells also tested as highly estrogen positive, perhaps near 100%.

For what it's worth, one doctor told me he thought the research institution was by far the most reliable and said the first company (the 20% report) was not highly respected. Yet here we had a major medical facility in State #2 using that company. And I just did some poking around on the Internet, and that company is growing by leaps and bounds. Our tax dollars, our insurance premiums, and our healthcare cost-sharing programs are funding that growth. Cancer is big business, and projected to grow like crazy. But it's our money. And at least in my case, their inaccurate analysis pushed me onto a very expensive treatment, the next step in the standard protocol.

Someone needs to figure this out—are we seeing incompetence or corruption?

I told Onc #2 about the 90% and she never acted like she cared, maybe because standard protocol is the only thing that matters. I can't think of another reason why a doctor would refuse to discuss a safer and more effective treatment for a patient.

Regarding this worsening abdominal pain, it was important to discover the cause—cancer growth or the cancer drugs? I now know it's possible with immunotherapy to get what's called hyper-progression, which apparently means the drugs are causing the cancer to progress more quickly. No one had warned me of this possibility. But if the pain was from the drugs, that was also an urgent issue—the drug sheets warned you could literally get a tear in your intestine! Talk about an emergency!

Because Onc #2 was so disinterested in my misery, I tried to ask logical probing questions: "What I want to know is, what does the abdomen feel like right before you get that intestinal tear? I want to know before it happens to avert a catastrophe."

Onc #2 didn't know and didn't seem to care. So I turned to my GP. Maybe she would help me. She was at a different medical institution, so she should've had the freedom to do what she wanted.

Yes! She was willing to order tests to find the cause of my pain. We started with a sonogram. Not much learned there, so MRI was next—with no need for gadolinium. Great, because you know how I feel about gadolinium. But the day before the MRI, I got an automated message that my MRI was cancelled. When I called to find out what had happened, the nurse on the phone said staff at THAT institution had decided to consult with Onc #2 at the other institution, and ONC #2 TOLD THEM NOT TO DO THE TEST!

Why would she do that? And no one called to talk with me!

The nurse on the phone was sympathetic: "You should be able to have any test you want. And it's obvious your insurance approved it, or it never would have been scheduled! Do you want me to reschedule it?" I said yes.

That night, I showed my roommate my belly. She had been a licensed practical nurse. With her experienced eyes she took one look and said, "That's fluid!"

*Oh, no.* Was it cancer progression? My daughter found a research article saying ascites fluid could come from the drugs! I NEEDED TO KNOW! If your cancer is progressing, you and your doctor are NOT supposed to stand around and wait for you to go past the point of no return! What was going on here?

I complained to another consulting doctor in a different state via video chat. She was also concerned. Out of desperation I said, "Do you know of ANY good oncologist ANYWHERE IN THIS ENTIRE COUNTRY?"

"Well, there's MY oncologist," she offered. He was a gastrointestinal oncologist. He didn't have expertise in gynecological cancer, but he was used to working in the abdomen, so I figured he would do. That's how desperate I was! **I just wanted someone who cared about my welfare!** So I started the paperwork.

A few days later, I got a phone call. My MRI was once again cancelled. I was told the imaging department said I could only have an MRI of the liver, but WITH GADOLINIUM! I said "No thanks," and got off the phone.

Then it hit me: *Wait a minute! There's no one in imaging who's going to practice medicine and tell me what I can or cannot have.* I called back to question the nurse. Sure enough, the previous caller had lied. Onc #2 had vetoed the test again! SHE was the one making these decisions, again without talking to me. She didn't know it right then, but she was fired! I packed my bags and was soon headed to another state.

# 21

## Cancer—State #3

I got an extended stay type of room with kitchen facilities. My health was quickly declining, but Onc #3 did a wonderful job of fitting me into his schedule and getting things done.

The only problem was he did not know much about ascites abdominal fluid. When he first touched my belly, I warned him, "I usually have a flat belly, so this is not normal for me."

As he pulled his hand away he snapped, "Give me some credit for being able to tell the difference between fluid and a fat belly!" **He said he did not think I had fluid, and he did not want to order the procedure called paracentesis, which inserts a needle into the abdomen to try to extract fluid.**

Meanwhile, I began to visit the cash-pay doctor who had recommended him. As his patient, she had put in a good word for me, which was why I saw him so quickly. Talking with her was my only other human connection at first, but I quickly found a supportive church.

I had my next immunotherapy with Onc #3, because we had not formulated another plan. They had done an amazing job of getting insurance approvals. Lightning fast!

Meanwhile, my abdominal discomfort was worsening. Eventually, things were so bad I had trouble eating—my stomach felt compressed. Then one day, I tried to lie on my back for a certain treatment at the cash-pay doctor's office, and I couldn't breathe: The fluid was pressing on my diaphragm. I couldn't finish the treatment. I was close to tears—I was so tired of being miserable for months and no one doing anything!

The following Monday, I told Onc #3 about it. He finally was willing to order a paracentesis. I pushed the hospital for fast service and got there two days later. They extracted 2.5 liters!

One of the nurses said, "When I first looked at you, I thought we'd get maybe one liter, but we got 2.5."

"Yeah," I said. "I've been trying to warn everyone you can't go by how I look."

Of course I never gave Onc #3 an "I told you so," but I hope he felt humbled once he saw the report. I don't know if he knew this, but the most fluid they remove at any one time from gynecological cancer patients is three or 3.5 liters, so 2.5 is a big deal.

The problem was, the fluid had a way of quickly coming back. I could only make it two days before I needed another paracentesis to be able to eat and avoid pain. Onc #3 just prescribed oxycodone for pain, but it was slow to kick in, so I would be in hell if I waited until I was sure I needed it. But I thought, *Who wants to become addicted to opioids or suffer the horrific side effects?* So I waited and suffered.

The pain became so bad that I'd curl up on my hotel bed and moan, and the opioid wasn't enough of a help, so I made a middle-of-the-night drive to the ER. But the ER staff wasn't trained to perform paracentesis, so I was told to wait until staff was available. They offered me morphine, but I declined—I didn't realize they meant I would wait for first shift! After a couple hours of waiting, I realized the situation and told the front desk employee I would take the morphine.

But they took their sweet time—more hours ticked by until I was rocking back and forth on my hard plastic chair and moaning. The other patient nearby and the desk employee ignored me. When I'd had all I could take, I stood up and asked the employee when I was going to get my morphine. Here I was, a woman who did not like ANY pharmaceutical drug, and I was begging for morphine!

Finally, they called me back and gave me the injection. *Ah, relief!* They sat me in a wheelchair and wheeled me back to the lobby, where I dozed off. When first shift arrived, I got my paracentesis. They told me they had to stop at three liters.

After that night, I tried pushing for more on a regular basis but still could only get one every four days. That meant I could eat during the first two days, but not the next two, and I'd be writhing in pain by the time I went to the next paracentesis. But AFTER the procedure, and even as that fluid was first starting to go down, I would return to my cheerful self. Such relief! Such joy! I would express such gratitude toward the professionals who worked on me. One day I said to them, "Man! You must have a very rewarding job! People come in so miserable and because of you they leave feeling so relieved and grateful!"

"Oh, you'd be surprised," they said. "We usually don't get appreciative customers." *Huh.*

Meanwhile, I was urgently thinking through my plan. Before immunotherapy, Dr. Cutting Edge had told me about a newer drug called Enhertu. It was successful with HER2-positive breast cancer and could now be used for other kinds of HER2-positive cancer. Or, he said another good option was to use the real Herceptin/trastuzumab to fight the HER2, along with an anti-estrogen drug such as Letrozole.

He seemed to favor attacking both the HER2 and the estrogen. "Why not go for the low-hanging fruit?" he reasoned.

It was obvious I needed a new plan—immunotherapy was failing me. As I later learned, research had already suggested that immunotherapy didn't work if the patient had taken antibiotics or lacked a gut bacterium called Akkermansia muciniphilla. Later, from a test ordered by a functional doctor, I learned BOTH were true for me. But when traditional medicine doesn't know and follow the research, patients get sent through treatments destined to fail. My microbiome should have been fixed first.

**So somewhere in that period of time, I hit another one of those breaking points: "No! Not doing this anymore!" I'd had enough of their standard protocol. DONE! It was literally killing me!**

I told Onc #3 I wanted to "go for the low hanging fruit" with the real trastuzumab/Herceptin and Letrozole. He tried to talk me out of it: "Right now, you're trying to get across a big river, and you need a motorboat to do that. Just using Herceptin and Letrozole would be like trying to paddle your way across with an inflatable raft!"

He was telling me I needed something with major killing power—a chemo. He pushed for the next drug in the standard protocol,

Doxorubicin. I did my research—low response rate and a high percent of women had adverse events severe enough to end up in the hospital. *Nope! Not having it!*

And I was in such bad shape that I thought, *I've got to make the drive to my daughter while I still can!* That meant State #4. So a dear friend from State #2 and church friends in State #1 helped me move. My daughter had found me an apartment, so all I had to do was roll into town and move in.

# 22

# Cancer—State #4

As I made that three-day trip, I worked the phone and email to push the bureaucracy to get started ASAP with Onc #4. I told the institution, "Assign me to someone who doesn't mind a patient doing her own research and thinking for herself!"

That's what I got, and I APPRECIATE HER SO MUCH! She is in traditional oncology, but she was willing to work with me in a respectful way. She of course pushed for the same standard protocol, but I told her I had seen the research, and I saw no sense in that—I wanted trastuzumab/Herceptin and Letrozole.

Medicare or the clinic—not sure which—would again force me to take a cheaper substitute for Herceptin from the trastuzumab family of drugs, but this time, rather than Kanjinti, it would be a different competitor. My attitude by then on that topic: *Whatever*. Again, I knew to pick my battles.

Early on, I had to see a doctor to discuss drug side effects, and in the waiting room, they handed me a survey: "What do you believe about your cancer?" There were boxes to check. One said something like, "I understand I won't be cured." Another, "I am uncertain whether I can be cured." I skipped the checkboxes and wrote in the white space: **"You would have to be ignorant of spiritual and psychological forces to say ANYTHING is incurable."**

I knew about scientific research on the power of the human mind, and I also knew of miraculous healings taken by faith. I have seen videos in which the individuals show their photos or medical records and even have their doctor appear on camera. I am convinced something is happening. But sometimes we feel unworthy of the miracle due to past trauma, or we might have fear and unbelief mixed with our faith. **Healing is a path of spiritual growth, a reprogramming of the mind.**

In the next few days I pushed the slow-moving bureaucracy. But our plan was set at that first appointment—I would get the cheaper trastuzumab and Letrozole. Dr. Cutting Edge and I thought that was the best option my local institution was offering at that time.

Meanwhile, I was fighting to get a paracentesis twice a week in this new state. Each time, they'd remove the maximum amount of fluid and express fear of throwing off my body's biochemistry. That might be why I woke up one morning with the room spinning and my heart rate sky high. For the first time in my life, I called an ambulance.

I went to the ER, and long story short, I ended up in worse shape. They had given me drugs and infusions that were backfiring. I was even dizzier than before, and now I was vomiting. When my daughter arrived, we decided we'd pressure the hospital to admit me. We had a good argument—how could they send me home when I couldn't even keep water down, and something THEY DID had caused it? We needed to figure this out, and I needed to stabilize.

So I spent the weekend in the hospital and made good use of my time. I pushed for another paracentesis while I was just lying there doing nothing. I also knew I'd need a baseline echocardiogram because all anti-HER2 drugs, such as the trastuzumab family and Enhertu, carry a risk of heart damage. So I asked the hospital doctor to order that for me. Getting the echo done that weekend expedited everything.

After that lovely detour, I refocused on my paracentesis schedule while looking ahead to my first drug treatment. I knew it was a dangerous gamble, because there would be no chemo to dramatically swoop in and rescue me from all those cancer cells. The trastuzumab biosimilar and Letrozole would be a more gradual process.

Was I too far gone? Was Onc #3 right—I needed a motorboat, not an inflatable raft? I did not know, but I had to go with my gut and follow the Spirit. We can't predict what the next twist or turn will be, so we have to walk in faith, not knowing what's next. But I had seen the research—I had a peace about refusing standard protocol.

As the days went by, I resolved that my paracentesis schedule was intolerable. For one thing, I needed to eat to fight cancer. I was now skin and bones. Second, I could no longer tolerate the torturous routine—two normal days followed by two days of hell caused by fluid accumulation.

At one of my paracentesis appointments, another one of those angels mentioned a PleurX drain that could be installed into my abdomen so that I could drain the fluid myself as needed. So I pushed for that. Onc #4 resisted. I suppose there's always pressure to control costs, but all those paracentesis appointments cost a lot of money too! I won that battle, and the surgery was ordered, but their bureaucracy scheduled that surgery for the DAY BEFORE my cancer treatment! I wanted at least a few days to heal, so I fought that battle and got the date changed.

In the first day or two with the drain in my abdomen, it was obvious to me I needed to be pumping daily, because I needed to be able to eat and avoid pain, and by then I could easily remove ONE LITER PER DAY, which was the capacity of those non-reusable vacuum bottles. But Onc #4 wanted every other day.

I recruited the home healthcare nurse who trained me on the use of the drain to argue on my behalf. Through her, I sent this message: "You're starving me to death!" That worked. And it was true. Once I could pump daily, I could eat as I should, and I never again messed up my biochemistry with those drastic reductions in body fluid.

Cancer-drug day was approaching, and when the oncology team met to discuss my case, they must have said, "We shouldn't allow this." We can be sure of that, because one week before treatment day, Onc #4 called me and said there's "a new drug" she'd like to recommend, called Enhertu.

*Oh! Someone is now going to make that available to me. Interesting!* I told her I was familiar with it, had researched it eight months earlier. I said I'd take a second look and let her know. My daughter and I looked again: No guarantees but good reason for hope. I knew I had my answer and dropped my other plan. So another round of going to war!

For most of 2023, I was on Enhertu, along with sporadic use of Letrozole, my choice. My plan also included holistic strategies—fasting for chemo, strict diet, wise exercise, drinking two or three quarts of water per day, good sleep, toxin avoidance, prayer—including group prayer for protection from side effects, and more.

Things went great. After the first treatment, both my high-tech circulating tumor DNA test and my low-tech marker used by traditional oncology crashed downward. The numbers were dropping every three weeks. The fluid in my belly was dropping too. Soon I could only extract 3/4 of a liter, then 1/2, then 1/3. Then I switched to every other day. I just went by how I felt. Then every third day. Then I waited a week—and still only 1/3 of a liter. Six days later, only one tablespoon! A week later just a couple drops. A whole week after that, just one teeny tiny air bubble.

Pop! That was it. **I had found my motorboat.**

One side effect was extreme hair thinning. I didn't go completely bald as I had in State #1, but my hair became so thin and scraggly that I looked ill, even when I felt fine. In fact, one day, I decided not to wear my wig to a doctor appointment—some days I just didn't care what I looked like—and when I checked in at the front desk, the receptionist took one look at me and asked me if I needed a wheelchair. I smiled and said, "No, thanks." I later told my friends, "Now THAT'S a bad hair day—when they take one look at you and offer you a wheelchair!"

One other effect was that my heart's left ventricular ejection fraction (LVEF) had dropped. Still in the normal range, but edging down near the danger zone. As you know, heart damage was a risk with this drug. So I had to decide when to get off Enhertu to protect my heart and the rest of my body. Traditional oncology would NEVER tell me to get off. Their advice was just keep going until the cancer develops resistance and the drug stops working, or until I was so damaged from chemo that I was forced off.

I'm not joking. That really was the standard advice.

From consulting yet another non-traditional doctor, I knew there was a sweet spot with Enhertu, according to the clinical experience treating breast cancer. The sweet spot was 6–12 months—

maximum benefit but less risk of heart damage. I decided to bail out at nine months. I had received a few negative circulating tumor DNA tests, my low-tech test was down near my all-time low, and my recent MRI imaging was clear. Good enough for me!

Later, when I checked in with Onc #4, she told me, "When I met you a year ago, I never would have predicted this. Most women in your situation are gone within a year."

Perhaps she did not realize it, but she was admitting to the disastrous track record of standard protocol. I was the first patient to use Enhertu there, only because I refused the standard protocol.

Now I try to do all I can, but I often fall short and fail to do all that I know to do. I'm working on my self-discipline—MAKING MYSELF take a break from things I love such as writing to you, and instead going out for more exercise and sunshine. Permanent remission is an ongoing challenge. This is not just cancer we're talking about, but STAGE-FOUR cancer, and a very aggressive one. But I have more knowledge now and am learning more all the time, and I've come to believe that cancer—along with all other chronic disease—is preventable AND REVERSIBLE for many of us, with the right strategies.

And I've been on a faith journey. I am learning to TUNE IN and TRUST. Will I tune in enough? Will I trust enough? Those are the questions I now must answer. Follow my progress on my website!

*Spirit*

# 23

# Basic Concepts

For the longest time I wondered what this section would be like. I was drawing a blank. I didn't feel qualified or worthy: *Who am I to write on this topic? I have no appropriate credentials, for one thing. My experience as a chaplain assistant isn't enough.*

But then it hit me: This section is no different from any other part of this book—all I can do is tell MY STORY and explain how things look to me. That's all ANY of us can do on ANY topic. None of us is an infallible god with an absolute lock on truth.

I also worried about what writing this book might cost me. Like Jane McLelland, I knew I'd been on a traumatic journey. I did not want to revisit all that, and unlike Jane, I'm not out of the woods yet. I imagine it was easier for her to go back through all that, knowing she was definitely a long-term cancer survivor. But could I afford RIGHT NOW the stress hormones of thinking back through all that?

In the next few weeks, as I sought Holy Spirit guidance, I became more and more sure I should proceed. If I had a calling, I should obey no matter what.

I felt stress remembering certain doctors, and I cried just a bit over my childhood, and I cried EVERY TIME when I read that scene in the play *Our Town*. I so much wish everyone could learn to appreciate life and each other!

Writing that section about *Our Town* kept bringing to mind the 1970 song by Joni Mitchell called "Big Yellow Taxi." The line I love is, "Don't it always seem to go that you don't know what you've got 'til it's gone?" We could say that's the theme of that scene in *Our Town*. Why do we humans wait until it's too late to properly appreciate what we had?

So what should I say about the Spirit portion of Mind-Body-Spirit wellness? Maybe the first thing is to acknowledge I've already started covering the spiritual life. It's impossible to cover the Mind and Body without recognizing a spiritual component—the psychological, physical, and spiritual are so interconnected! Even some researchers now realize that!

And maybe I've already made the best possible case for authentic Christianity by illustrating the terrible pain we suffer when humans can't treat each other well. I'm sad to say we live in a culture where people are too often self-absorbed, unwilling to help others unless pressured or paid, unwilling to see their own faults and mistakes, unwilling to do the difficult and courageous work of changing the world—who wants to live with any of that? But authentic Christianity is a remedy for ALL of that.

I personally lean toward spiritual concepts that are universal, sort of like laws of nature. To explain a concept, I sometimes refer to the law of gravity as a good analogy. We know here on Earth we'll be affected by gravity. You can believe gravity doesn't exist if you want to, but good luck when you jump off that 10-story building!

And so it is with other universal laws, such as the law of "karma," or as some say, "What goes around, comes around," or as the Bible says, "As you sow, so shall you reap." It's a universal law, and that's easier to see as we observe the LONG TERM. We might think someone got away with something, but that's where our understanding of life must expand, must cross to a more spiritual dimension, as our eyes are opened to both subtle and long-term impact, even multi-generational impact.

I like to say I'm a follower of Jesus Christ. But I'm shy about saying I'm "Christian," because so many people claim to be Christian when their behavior casts doubt on that. I've been hurt and even traumatically wounded by people who claimed to be Christian. And just as Jesus explained, it is often the rules-obsessed or those with a superior attitude that are the worst.

Back in HIS day, Jesus would patiently set them straight, or become exasperated and criticize them to their face, or even resort to name-calling! So don't let anyone paint a picture of Jesus as this passive wimp. He was a tough guy in the best sense of that phrase, and he sure wasn't afraid of rocking the boat. In fact, one of my favorite memes is the one that says, "If anyone asks you 'What would Jesus do?' remind him that flipping over tables and chasing people with a whip is within the realm of possibilities." Ha! So true!

To accompany Francis Chan's comment about 90% of people in church not being Christian, here's one of my favorite quotations, from the theologian G.K. Chesterton: "The Christian ideal has not been tried and found wanting. It has been found difficult and left untried."

Those are strong words, and I can't speak for him, but I doubt he meant that NO ONE has tried it. None of us should devalue all those great heroes of world history, all the self-sacrificing, loving individuals, all the wise leaders who fought for a worthy cause. At the risk of omitting so many other worthy examples, I'm thinking of the Christian abolitionists, both white and black, who risked their lives to run the Underground Railroad, helping slaves escape to freedom.

In a similar vein, I'm thinking of Elijah Parish Lovejoy, a white pastor and newspaper editor who persisted in printing an abolitionist newspaper despite many threats and acts of violence against him and his printing press. Ultimately, after buying his FOURTH printing press if I counted correctly, he was murdered for his devotion to God, his condemnation of slavery, and his dogged insistence on free speech. But his death ignited the anti-slavery movement even more.

And I'm thinking of Robert Graetz, a white pastor who persisted in helping Martin Luther King Jr. in the Montgomery Bus Boycott, despite threats and actual violence. I read that he and his wife, Jeannie, had their home bombed twice, among other things.

And I'm thinking of John Quincy Adams, known mostly for being the sixth President of the United States, but who also worked for decades to end slavery. The explanation for his persistence is perhaps found in his statement, **"Duty is ours, results are God's."** Perhaps you'll recall that I expressed—in different words—the same idea earlier in this book, but I'd never heard this quotation from Adams until yesterday.

But I'm not just thinking of famous people. I'm also thinking of all the self-sacrificing parents and grandparents. And the countless volunteers in nonprofit organizations. And all the loving people who have listened, encouraged, and mentored others, leaving a legacy that continues on through countless generations. And on and on we could go.

So while I don't think Chesterton meant to disparage all the great Christians of human history, I do love the point that I think he was making, which is that authentic Christianity is challenging, and yes, even difficult, and thus RELATIVELY RARE. This is actually STATED in scripture, as Jesus told the crowd:

> "Enter through the narrow gate. For wide is the gate and broad is the road that leads to destruction, and many enter through it. But small is the gate and narrow the road that leads to life, and only a few find it" (Matthew 7:13-14 NIV).

It seems Jesus meant avoiding the EASY path in life, which is so tempting, so easy to fall into, but which leads to destruction, and instead choosing the more challenging path—the one that might bring more pain and suffering, but will also prove to be the only path to a successful, happy, fulfilled life. That takes some courage, some grit.

That need for courage is another universal law. The author Brené Brown has said her research shows the ONLY path to love and connection is to be of COURAGE and to understand the POWER OF VULNERABILITY. Choosing to be vulnerably honest and transparent sure does take courage!

I've also mentioned a call to greatness, where we MAKE OURSELVES DO THE RIGHT THING, despite our fears or our preference for comfort and convenience: "Feel the fear and do it anyway."

But sometimes fear is a valid warning. Challenging yourself—learning to tell the difference—is an important part of spiritual growth.

Some people think courage is a LACK of fear. While it's true that certain people have reported performing a heroic act without taking time to feel fear, I think it's more common that we feel the fear and push ourselves through. Ordinary examples include speaking up for what's right, offering an invitation despite fear of rejection, working toward success against the odds, and so on.

Some Christians try to say we don't deserve ANY credit for our courage or persistence—that's the Holy Spirit within us. I understand where they are coming from theologically and their fear of the sin of pride, but I think they have let their pendulum swing too far to one side. While it's true we can draw strength and courage from the Holy Spirit, we ALSO have free will, the freedom to choose. We can choose to be brave, or we can choose to be cowardly. We can choose to seek Holy Spirit guidance, or we can choose to plunge forward recklessly.

Any extreme philosophy that would deny that power to choose makes no sense to me. We are not lifeless puppets, waiting for God or the Holy Spirit to start pulling our strings marionette-style, MAKING us say and do the right thing. If that's how it was, there'd be no point in Jesus giving instructions in a sermon, because we couldn't obey—we'd be sitting there, just powerless puppets, waiting for God to act through us.

So no, I would say it's not either God or us. It's both-and. We form a partnership. Likewise, I wouldn't feel sympathy if someone tried to claim, "The devil made me do it." As I said, I'm a big believer in personal responsibility, and I'm distressed that our culture has drifted away from this concept.

If you're younger than I am, you may not even realize the cultural trend in which you've been ensnared. But way back when I started out as a high school teacher, my school superintendent complained, "We are now in the era of all rights and no responsibilities!" He had such accurate vision! There has been a downward cultural slide ever since, and I think everyone is now feeling the effects. As a society, we must heed warnings EARLY ON and use wisdom, rather than listen to the voices sowing division in order to divide and conquer.

Where will you seek this wisdom, this resistance to evil manipulation? How will you cut through the confusion? How will you find enlightenment?

Ancient sources of wisdom such as the Bible can free you from having to learn everything in life the hard way—no need to attend The School of Hard Knocks. You won't have to struggle to figure everything out from scratch, reinventing the wheel every day of your life. Would any rational person think that thousands of years of human wisdom have nothing useful to offer?

You can learn vicariously through all the screw-ups made by individuals in the Bible. And believe me, there were plenty of them! Some people think the Bible is just an account of saintly people. Ha! Of course there are those who stepped forward to do a saintly thing, but scripture is at least X-rated, and many of those people had previously been murderers, adulterers, liars, cowards, thieves, and more. So the good news is, it doesn't matter what our past looks like. A new and better life is waiting for us.

But I digress! The concept of free will makes perfect sense to me. If there really were a God creating a world with His people, He'd HAVE TO give free will. What good would it do to be loved by mindless robots with no choice? That's an unsatisfying, meaningless concept.

Here's another universal law—the law of letting go of a desperate desire to control, granting others freedom to choose. The act of letting go is also an act of love and reverence. I'm reminded of what psychologist Dr. Joy Brown used to say in her radio broadcast: "We parents give our children roots and wings, and the hard part is not the roots."

So helping to develop those "wings," and then letting go, is an act of courage, faith, and trust, and a deep respect and love for the one being released. Parents understand how hard those moments can be, and are likely to cry just thinking back. They have a sense of joy and pride but also sadness and loss. An era has ended and a new time has begun. It doesn't matter whether we're thinking back to the day our children first climbed on the school bus, or we said goodbye as they shipped out with the military, or we dropped them off for the first time at college and drove home to an empty nest, or we watched them walk down the aisle. Many of the emotions are the same, and it takes courage to let go.

Perhaps it is similar with God, who lovingly bestows free will and lets go, knowing that His children are likely to fall down sometimes and hurt themselves, and yes, even reject Him. But there's no other good way.

This concept of a LOVING relationship is an especially important one. Many, many people have been misinformed, in my opinion, and have been taught to think that, to be Christian, one must EARN God's love, acceptance, and approval. I've been taught that's sort of an Old Testament mentality. I've heard authentic Christianity is unique in that there's no need to EARN that sense of belonging, no need to strive to be good enough. Because perfection is not possible, there is no such thing as "good enough." That rules-based, earning perspective comes from a time when the ancient Hebrews were given a long list of rules and laws, and the task was set before them to try to follow them all. Setting people up for failure has one major advantage—it becomes painfully obvious to the humans that they need some help outside themselves.

We are not perfect. We are not infallible gods. We need something outside ourselves. Even if we choose to have nothing to do with Christianity or any other religion, we'd still better understand that!

It's a universal truth that we aren't 100% the be-all and end-all, completely self-sufficient. As I said in the Mind section, understanding that is the antidote to narcissism.

So in the New Testament, a new covenant or agreement is established between God and all people. The first principle remains the same—the universe must continue to operate with love and mercy on the one hand and justice on the other. Both must be present for optimum human life.

We can easily understand this idea when we consider the parental role: If parents are ONLY love and mercy, they spoil the child and create a monster. Two-year-olds are natural narcissists: They want what they want, and they want it now, and they might have a temper tantrum if they don't get it. They need to learn there's a world outside of them, and a system of justice, unwritten rules for what's right and fair, and that includes the rights of others. Woe to the parent who caters to the little prince or princess and never teaches this concept of self-discipline! That is not just a crime against humanity—that's also a crime against the child. That child is headed for one miserable life.

So in the NEW covenant, this need for justice remains, but in an act of love, the METHOD of justice is changed. God ends the religious practice of animal sacrifice and instead offers HIMSELF as the one final, sufficient sacrifice for all sin—past, present, and future. It is an act of great love and a push for true intimacy, a removal of the barrier or separation between God and humankind.

We can also understand THIS concept of great intimacy if we imagine two spouses, and one has damaged the relationship. Doing what it takes to establish a clean slate allows the couple to grow close once again and leave behind that damage and emotional distance. They are once again united in mind and heart.

People who have been through that healing process understand that experience as one of the greatest feelings ever.

And so it is with God. In an act of great sacrificial love, for the sake of that intimate connection, God offers Himself, otherwise known as "His Son." This concept strikes many as weird, but is easier to understand if we know in Jesus's day, fathers and sons were considered the same identity in many respects—destined to work in the exact same business, travel similar paths in life, and maintain a multi-generational legacy. Because Jesus claimed to be the same as "The Father," and was understood to be God in fleshly form ("Emmanuel" from the Greek, meaning "God with us"), we can understand that God is offering HIMSELF in order to create a close, healed relationship with us human beings.

So the sacrifice, in which Jesus voluntarily bore all sin and disease and was crucified, is called the atonement for sin. The word "sin" comes from an archery term that means "missing the mark." In other words, the word "sin" simply means ANY falling short of perfection.

I think this idea of atonement is beautifully explained with this analogy:

> A judge is saddened to see his good friend before him in the courtroom, charged with a crime and definitely guilty. Because the judge can't violate the law, he has to pronounce his friend guilty and impose a fine, a fine that his friend would never be able to pay. But then, after imposing the fine, the judge stands up, takes off his robe, comes down from the bench, and pays the fine.

This is what Jesus did. Just like the judge's payment of the fine, that act of generosity is a free gift that offers a better future, and the chance to move forward in friendship. The friend just needs to understand and accept the gift, or it doesn't work. If the friend is in denial and says he has no guilt, it also doesn't work.

## *The Heart and the Healthy Balance*

Now, I'm not saying that Jesus completely rejected all religious laws. He emphasized the heart had to be one of love and compassion and humility, but never compassion to the point of enabling wrongdoing. Life is a pursuit of that healthy middle zone. That can feel like walking a tightrope as we deal with people, trying to move forward without leaning too far to one side or the other. Fall off to one side and your excess mercy enables wrongdoing and generates future misery for more people. But fall off to the other side and you come down too hard on people with hasty judgments or harsh condemnation.

## *A Loving God*

Many people have rejected Christianity with this thought: *How could I ever accept a God who causes babies to die, children to have cancer, and so many people to suffer? If that's who God is, I want nothing to do with that!*

I think I understand the origin of that misunderstanding: I've spent years in churches that retained a fearful Old Testament mentality—expecting or fearing disasters, perhaps seeing disasters as punishment from God or as God's attempt to force people into growth. This mindset creates a tremendous amount of insecurity—a lack of trust.

A perfect example of Old Testament insecurity is King David's desperate pleading in some of the psalms. Seems he was wrestling with his own view of God. But in his defense, that was a time BEFORE the sacrifice of Jesus and the creation of a new covenant. To those who accept the sacrificial gift, there's a new identity and bold confidence as a cherished son or daughter of God and a new reason to relax and trust in God's care and provision, as God forgets our sin and sees us through the righteousness of Jesus. As a loving father, God WANTS you to find joy in life, God WANTS you to be healthy, God WANTS you to have long life, God WANTS you to prosper. As Jesus said, "…I have come that they may have life, and have it in all its fullness" (John 10:10 BSB).

Jesus wasn't just talking about getting a ticket to an afterlife, according to what I've learned. He was talking about having an abundant, meaningful, purpose-filled, joy-filled life here on Earth, with a peace of mind that surpasses all understanding. And there are other scriptures that support this view.

That doesn't mean there won't be heartache, because there are evil forces, and laws of biochemistry and physics and other laws of nature, and we live in a world of free will with both purposeful human sin and accidental human mistakes. But as I now understand, it's not accurate to blame God for the suffering in the world. And this is going to sting for some people, but I have come to realize THAT philosophy, which says that God is behind every tragedy, is sometimes a cover for a lack of personal responsibility or a lack of faith:

**Lack of Personal Responsibility:** If we eat poorly and fail to exercise, we can't blame our type 2 diabetes or other disease on "God's will." It's also NOT OUR FAULT if we didn't know any better. But once we've been warned, then we need to accept personal responsibility.

**Lack of Faith:** Here's another idea that might sting, but I finally came to a fork in the road where I had to choose: Am I going to believe what Jesus said? Or am I going to persist in a watered-down, powerless, faithless, man-made version of Christianity, which ignores the importance of taking everything by faith and learning how to walk in faith?

Even researchers understand the unbelievable power of the human mind to change physical reality. Maybe it's time that some Christians catch up to the researchers—ironically enough—and take seriously the Holy Spirit power that Jesus said His believers would be granted! If we don't really believe what Jesus said, we limit our own faith—we confine ourselves to saying people get "saved by faith," because their arrival in heaven can't be tested and proven. But if we believe what Jesus ACTUALLY SAID, and we say that faith can even HEAL a person, for example—which is pretty much what science is discovering—well, now we have something that can be proven here on Earth!

So when something goes wrong, as one pastor explained, they try to spare people's guilty feelings and end up blaming God: "Well, it must have been God's will." But that maligns God's true character! In the Bible I see a Jesus who was ALWAYS willing to heal, so I don't think it's right to blame God. There are so many other factors!

So this negative view of God can still be found in some churches. That negativity is also found in the broader culture—consider the fact that insurance companies might refer to a flood, tornado, hurricane, or earthquake as "an act of God." Isn't it amazing how our attitudes might be shaped without our even realizing it?

Some might argue that God is still to blame because he ALLOWS bad things to happen. They argue that God is "almighty" and "sovereign" and therefore CONTROLS EVERYTHING.

But does He? What about free will? God perhaps desires that all people be "saved" or that all people avoid sin, but he obviously doesn't control that. Maybe we should say he CHOSE NOT TO CONTROL when he first created the world.

So that's MY newer view—a loving God. But I can testify: Keeping unbelief out of our minds is one of the hardest things, ESPECIALLY when we're facing an imminent tragedy like stage-four cancer. But help is available to us. Here's one of my favorite verses, spoken by a man asking Jesus to heal his son: "...I do believe, but help me overcome my unbelief" (Mark 9:24 New Living Translation).

Another one of those paradoxes! We can have faith, but is it mixed with fearful unbelief? Here's an illustration that I love:

> A high-wire artist is crossing the Niagara Falls by walking on a cable stretched across the river. He can even push a heavily loaded wheelbarrow in front of him as he crosses. He turns to someone who has been watching and asks, "Do you believe I can safely cross again with this wheelbarrow?" The observer enthusiastically says yes. The high-wire artist says, "Okay, get in." *Uh, no, thanks!*

What a gut check! Do we really believe? I mean REALLY believe! What a challenge sometimes! But the good news is we can ask for help to renew our minds. Faith comes by hearing the Word of God, by speaking that scripture—praying it aloud, and by choosing to believe and then stepping out in faith. It is a learning process, a conditioning of the mind, dwelling on the promises of God, leaving no room for doubt and fear.

Easier said than done, but I'm working on that. Like almost everything in life, faith development takes time. We're foolish to wait for that cancer diagnosis or other emergency before developing faith—not that things can't work out, but man, is that making life more difficult—to wait until a crisis is upon us! Keeping the faith is a spiritual battle. The battlefield is my mind. But the Holy Spirit is there to help, if only I will believe and call out and claim Holy Spirit power. I am learning! Brick by brick, my friend!

This might sound strange, but sometimes I don't mind being challenged in this way. As I've said, life is a call to greatness. Adversity can create wonderful changes within. So we can build

THIS attitude: **The worse things get, the more I grow!** That's partly what I mean by, "We have the power to turn the world upside down." It's a new way of thinking. Are you starting to see your way through?

**All I can say is, I will give it everything I've got, and if things don't go the way I'd like, I won't be blaming God.**

# 24

# The Stumbling Block of Divinity

It's time to tackle the elephant in the room. I understand that many people doubt the possibility of a divine being. You may think the Bible is full of errors and mythology, and maybe you mistrust people who talk like they believe in anything transcendent. I understand more than you might think. I have been one of you at times, and to be painfully honest, maybe I still am in some ways.

I have reasons for my faith, but keeping a hold on that faith is hard at times, especially when fear comes busting down my door! And don't forget, my father was an atheist. That certainly left a mark, once we kids grew older and he started expressing his true thoughts.

Experts say we tend to relate to God the way we related to our earthly father. So if our father was cruel, angry, or critical, growing some faith is perhaps going to be more of a challenge. Those of us who have been abused may see God as an angry God just waiting to hammer us with punishment. And those of us who have abandonment issues might struggle to believe in a loving God who is present with us, will never leave us or forsake us.

But the whole thing can be a challenge for ANYONE, especially when tragedy strikes. I think everyone hypothetically has a breaking point, at least for a brief moment. Some people just never get pushed to their limit, so they are untested, untried.

But for what it's worth, here are some ideas that resonate with me. They might not look theologically correct to some people—there are many different views of scripture. In all honesty, I'm not too concerned about anyone's approval, and I'm not entering into debates with anyone. **I just want to tell you from the heart about the real ME just in case you find a few helpful ideas.**

**I think I've reached this freer attitude of wanting to self-reveal but not worry about approval through my profound emotional healing and spiritual growth. Revealing myself to you is a by-product of my newer respect for myself and a natural outgrowth of my deep love for you.**

*Universal Laws*

We begin with what I've already covered. I see so many universal laws, so many true principles operating in this world of ours. What should we call the source of those laws? If you listen to a famous atheist or two, they might argue against any religion because of all the hatred and warfare that has come out of religious movements, and I share their outrage and their grief. But I can't help but wonder about their assertion that hatred and warfare are bad: Where did they get THAT idea? Why aren't they promoting an evolutionary "survival of the fittest"? On what basis do they insist there is any kind of moral value, such as avoiding hatred? Are THEY the lawgiver for the rest of us? If not, who is?

So I think they are kind of making my point: There are some universal principles and values operating here, and we all seem to know it, even those of us who claim no religion at all.

**Something That Endures**

So I know there's this "something," the source of these principles. And it seems to have longevity through the ages. Likewise, everything WE do creates a permanent change to human history—that ripple effect expanding forever. Especially when I consider that eternal impact, I CARE what my track record in life is like! I CARE how I treated people! And remember—we can convert evil to good in so many different ways. We can change the course of history by converting the bad to good when we are victimized. Then that GOOD is what lives on forever!

Once again, "we have the power to turn this world upside down!" The play *Our Town* makes some beautiful comments about the eternal—one reason to give copies as gifts!

**Simplicity as a Priority**

Many in the Christian world insist the Bible is without error. Some take many parts as literally true. Others interpret those parts as metaphorically true. There is diversity of thought. I don't have all the answers, and I'm perfectly fine with that, because my faith doesn't rely on my being correct about every little thing. I just like to keep the main thing the main thing.

I believe, if people would just focus on doing what Jesus told them to do, this world would be an amazingly better place. So my loyalty is to Jesus Christ, and Jesus Christ alone. I am NOT saying I disregard the rest. I'm saying I think I have my priorities straight, and I like knowing that ONE PERSON, Jesus, is where I rest my mind and heart and draw my core identity.

## Understanding Human Nature

The historical reliability of the Gospel accounts is discussed in the 2007 **documentary** *The Case For Christ* (not referring to the movie of the same name). One way or another, those accounts are eyewitness accounts. So can those eyewitnesses be trusted? The documentary addresses that.

Perhaps the biggest stumbling block is the idea of a resurrection. I have always been mindful of HUMAN NATURE: These disciples transformed from scared cowards, hiding from authorities and even betraying Jesus, to bold believers willing to DIE for speaking what they believed. I don't think humans make that switch without something profound happening. These people would have known if they were perpetuating a lie. And I think I know human nature well enough that people don't go out and die for an idea that they know is a hoax.

I also look at details in the accounts that don't square with a fictitious story. We see a view of the disciples that is often unflattering. They can appear at times to be stupid, prideful, impulsive, and more, and Jesus on occasion became frustrated with them and chewed them out. If people were going to tell a fictitious story, why wouldn't they have looked more saintly? And in the case of John, if you look closely, you can see humorous examples of his human pride. All of that, in my view, adds to the credibility of the story.

## A Counter-Cultural Revolution

I also find details that were not typical of the time, and still not typical when the first accounts must have been written—delightfully COUNTER-CULTURAL, in other words. One example is the mention of Mary Magdalene as one of the first to encounter the empty tomb and run to tell the disciples what she had seen. I've heard the word of a woman was not taken seriously back then, and yet here is a plot point that flies in the face of what you'd expect if people of that culture were constructing a nice story.

Oh, and by the way, I just learned you can't trust Google to give you a quick answer about the Bible: It says only the book of John mentions Mary Magdalene at the empty tomb. Not true. All four gospels do mention her, although Luke takes longer to mention her by name as one of "the women." Accounts can vary according to who is interviewed and who is writing the account, and that's ALWAYS true in life, even with eyewitness accounts.

And speaking of the role of women, I'm happy to report that Jesus was quite the "women's libber," to borrow a phrase from the 1960s and 70s. He treated women as equal to men in many surprising ways. For example, he defended a woman who chose to sit and learn from him rather than doing kitchen work. Sitting at the feet of, and learning from, the rabbi was a privilege accorded ONLY TO MEN in that day. And she was not the only example of women treated with special care or respect!

Even the apostle Paul, who is known for one or two comments that, out of context, might offend women, ALSO said, "There is neither Jew nor Greek, there is neither slave nor free, there is neither male nor female; for you are all one in Christ Jesus" (Galatians 3:28 New King James Version). That statement is understood to mean that all are of equal value.

We might look at the Judeo-Christian culture—along with much of the rest of the world in human history—and see women treated as property, or at least as second-class citizens. That certainly can turn people away from MANY religions!

**But here's something that might really rock your world:** If we look at scripture carefully enough, we can see God's INTENT, rather than just the HUMAN CORRUPTION that followed. For example, zoom in on Genesis 2:18, which describes the creation of

woman as a "helper" for man. Of course, translations vary, but we might examine these:
- "…I will make him a helper comparable to him." –NKJV
- "…suitable for him." –New American Standard Bible
- "…fit for him." –ESV

Those translations give us an adjective to describe what kind of helper. And then the literal translations say:
- "…a helper as his counterpart." –Literal Standard Version
- "…as before him." –Smith's Literal Translation
- "…a helper who is like him." –Lamsa Bible from Aramaic

And then we come to what I see as the final nail in the coffin for the idea that women were supposed to be inferior assistants or second-class citizens. We learn that the Hebrew word translated as "helper," which is "ezer," is also used three times in the Bible to refer to an army that serves as an ally in war, and **the remaining 16 times is used to refer to GOD! God, the one who saves and upholds mankind!** And the Hebrew word for "suitable" literally means "as in front of him," meaning standing face to face, of the same quality, not identical but complementing each other and of equal value.

Wow! Christianity, when ORIGINAL and AUTHENTIC, is one of the great forces to elevate women and women's rights. In my view, the opposite examples in Judeo-Christian history were men violating God's intent and violating what Jesus taught and demonstrated in his life. I myself have seen men cherry-pick the words of the apostle Paul: *You women need to pay attention to what Paul said here, but we men are going to ignore the even more important thing that Paul said to men right before that, which changes the meaning of the entire passage!*

**Oh, let me show you my shocked face—that some people claim to be Christian, but ignore what Jesus said and did. Ha!**

See my website to learn more or simply find encouragement and inspiration. I just think, if we're going to reject ANYTHING, we should have an ACCURATE view of what we're rejecting, for our own sakes. I don't think any of us want to be deceived or misled.

# 25

# Supernatural Experiences

Earlier I described a few moments that seemed supernatural, but now I'd like to share a few favorite and more significant examples. With my particular church background, I never would have expected supernatural experiences or miracles—nothing like that was ever discussed, even though the Bible is full of miracles, and Jesus promised we could perform miracles greater than what he had performed, by the power of the Holy Spirit. We'll start with just a few of the rain miracles in chronological order, which came during some very difficult years of my life.

One day when I was painting the house, I looked up and realized a storm was coming. I quickly put my equipment away and then, because it had not yet started raining, I thought I'd take the dog for a quick walk. I got about one block from my house, and the rain started sprinkling. I looked up and said, "God, if you could just protect my paint."

Instantly the sprinkling stopped, and I kept going with the dog. We did one quick trip around the block and then went inside. The rest of the day, we never got any rain.

I suppose anyone could say that alone was a miracle or answer to prayer, but I wouldn't at that point. But when I later chatted with a friend who lived one mile away, she told me the rain had POURED at her house! I assume that would make anyone sit up and take notice, but I didn't get TOO excited. It could have been coincidence, right?

On the next occasion, I headed to our local greenway for a jog. I knew from the online forecast that rain was on its way, but I hoped I'd have time to squeeze in a quick run. As I pulled into the parking lot, I was disappointed to see on my windshield that rain was starting. I said, "God, if you could just let me squeeze in this run."

I noticed as I shut off the ignition, the rain stopped. *Great*, I thought. *I'm going for it. Probably going to start again soon, but it won't kill me to get wet.*

With that thought, I decided to be daring and try for my typical distance. I wasn't much of a runner, so I was only running one mile out and walking the mile back, and I was slow. I knew the whole thing would take about a half hour. But I liked measuring my distance with the greenway mile markers, and I enjoyed relaxing on the walk back. I also strongly preferred this location because the trail was crushed limestone, and I'd already experienced touchy knees from running on concrete.

This time, feeling a bit nervous, I alternated walking with jogging on the way back to hasten my return. I was relieved when I made it back to my starting point, and the rain still had not come. I may have said a quick prayer of thanks, or knowing me, I probably didn't think anything divine was involved. *Maybe I was just lucky.* I headed back to my car.

Just as I opened my driver's door and precisely when my butt hit the seat, the rain started to fall on my windshield again. Now that really took me aback! I thought, *What are the odds?*

The next two, I was walking the dog at night in the neighborhood. The rain started to fall on us, and again, I felt free to ask God for a reprieve. The rain stopped instantly.

The next time was different in one way—same neighborhood, same time of day. I was walking the dog when a light rain started. THIS time, I had the sense that I was being told, "Just don't even ask." So I never asked and it kept raining. The dog and I continued for a minute and then hurried home. We were getting wet!

As time went on, I started to believe I wasn't MAKING these miracles occur, but rather it was a case of knowing whether or not I should ask, a sensing of the future.

One Sunday morning at church, a tornado came through the metro area. Hundreds of us had to go down to the basement and wait. After the all-clear, my friend and I lingered in the lobby for a few minutes to chat with people. The rain had completely stopped and the sun was out, so we decided to go to a restaurant several minutes down the road. Walking through the restaurant parking lot, I noticed the weather was still bright and shiny, though the pavement was wet and filled with puddles. When we entered the restaurant, the greeter said, "You gals must be living right! It was pouring here just a little while ago!"

At this point I had started to realize a pattern, and I was no longer surprised. As we enjoyed our lunch, I saw through the window that the dark skies and rain were back, but by the time we finished eating, it was once again bright and clear. I remember thinking, *Man, I'm kind of getting used to this!*

After that, I started to expect it, and I began to believe I could almost COUNT ON that special kind of "grace." I think I was still grateful and giving God credit, but I was also starting to take it for granted. I think it's hard for our human brains to see everything as fresh and new, as the play *Our Town* explains.

There were many more examples and never any exceptions during those years. On some errands, I'd back out of my garage into the rain, but by the time I exited my car to walk through the store parking lot, there was no need for an umbrella.

Later, I joined a Christian social group, and one night, I told the leader about these miracles. He was a good listener and seemed interested. This group had a paper newsletter, which he mailed out on a monthly basis. The next one I received had his handwritten note at the top: "If I ever need a rain miracle, I'm calling you, Carol."

A few weeks later, we were supposed to go hiking. Rain was predicted, and everyone in the online discussion agreed that if we got rained out, we'd meet at the restaurant we had planned to visit after the hike. I was SO TEMPTED to post a comment saying we did NOT have to worry about that rain. I wasn't dictating that—I was SENSING IT. Somehow, I just knew. But I chickened out and did not post anything. *What if I turn out to be wrong?*

So the day came, and I headed out to the state park. Even though it had not started to rain, I had seen comments that some were heading straight to the restaurant, but it was unclear what everyone else was doing, so I kept going to the state park.

Please trust me that I would not lie or exaggerate, and I'm not crazy: A mile or two from the state park entrance, it started to rain pretty good. Not super hard, but way more than a sprinkling. Significant. And here's the surprising part, especially for me: Rather than feeling relieved that I had never said anything to the group, or disappointed because rain was starting, I felt as certain as I could be that this rain was irrelevant, and I had a thought that was very strange for me. I thought, *No, this is going to glorify God.*

That is an expression used by Jesus and others meaning that something unlikely or miraculous would serve to prove who God is, demonstrate how great God is. BUT WHY WAS I THINKING THAT? I wasn't the type to sound so religious! But that's exactly what I thought, and I know it wasn't an act of MY WILL, but something that just came over me.

So I got to the entrance of the park and asked the attendant, "Can I enter for free since it's raining?" She said yes.

I pulled into a parking spot, and as I turned off the car THE RAIN STOPPED!

A couple pulled in next to me, so I approached their driver's door to ask if they were with the group. They were, so I started telling them about this rain miracle, plus a bit of the background. I didn't feel weird sharing that because this was a Christian group, but I could see skepticism in their faces. We chatted for a bit longer, and then they said it looked like no one else was coming, so they were heading to the restaurant.

As they left, I was thrilled to see the next car arrive, a young gal from the group. We waited a while and then decided no one else was coming. We did a hike through the woods for 20-30 minutes. At that point I was eager to join the group at the restaurant for some socializing. My companion said she didn't have the budget for a restaurant and wanted to keep hiking, so we parted ways. I crossed the field back to my van and headed out.

Just as I turned right, exiting the park and pulling onto the main road, IT STARTED TO RAIN with the same significant rainfall. I burst out crying, because I could not believe the timing. By the time I reached the restaurant, it had quit raining. No need for an umbrella, and no rain the rest of the night.

In this final example, I'd already been diagnosed with cancer and was in treatment. I exercised regularly at the YMCA and was driving the ten minutes over when it started raining. The Bible says we should not put the Lord our God to the test, and I don't know if this counts, but I thought, *God, if I'm going to be healed of this cancer, let it be a sign to me that the rain stops exactly when I park at the Y.*

For the next few minutes I felt nervous, but sure enough, the rain did stop exactly then, and I walked into the building with, as usual, no need for an umbrella.

Those are my favorite examples. Now, in these more recent years, I only recall four or five instances of rain falling on me. Am I back to normal percentages? What are normal percentages?

I'll finish this chapter with a few of my supernatural experiences that have nothing to do with rain.

### *Radio and TV*

Many times a "message" came through my car radio or television—someone making a comment out of the blue that was appropriate for my specific, difficult situation, like it was God talking to me. Many of those could be dismissed as coincidence if you listen to something inspirational such as Christian radio. But some of my examples were so specific and so against the odds that I broke down crying. It seemed God was reassuring me that everything would be okay.

My favorite example came during an extremely high-pressure situation. I was leaving an office building after conducting some business. In the lobby, I felt so stressed and overwhelmed that I squatted down and started reorganizing all my papers and the things in my purse. I had to make sure I had everything. I had to just stop and collect my wits. This was one of the worst times in my life, and I was close to the breaking point, where you collapse on the floor, like a horse that has been ridden and whipped until it finally lies down with the rider on, totally incapable of moving forward.

But I collected myself, walked up the street to the parking deck, and got in my car. When I turned the ignition, the car radio came on, and Mandisa sang, "He wants you to know you're an overcomer!" Another time when I burst out crying!

When I examined the song lyrics online, I saw something even more stunning. Not only had the timing been absolutely perfect, but that was the ONLY TIME when she sings those words. The phrase "you're an overcomer" occurs many times, but "He wants you to know" occurs only once. That song has been special to me ever since and has gotten me through my cancer journey.

The official "Overcomer" video features two famous cancer patients and two other famous overcomers. See my website for more tunes that offer hope and inspiration!

*Email*

Next, I was under great stress up against a deadline, watching for an email. I had spent probably two hours randomly checking my inbox, and as the deadline drew near, I was checking more and more often, until I was clicking constantly. I had never thought to pray. But then, I decided to pray for that email to arrive. Boom! There it was in literally the next second. Coincidence?

*Observation*

Now stranger things: One time, someone I knew needed to correct an individual who had been doing evil things, and I was there to observe. The conversation went fine—until it transitioned to the part this individual would NOT want to hear. I was stunned to see a dark gray shadow develop in front of this person's head and upper body. In my spirit, I felt I was seeing angry malevolence and an evil resistance to truth. The second the conversation moved on, the gray shadow disappeared.

*A Direct Message*

Another tense situation: It was late at night, and I had been searching for a piece of important information. I had given up looking and was resting on the couch in the dark and the silence. Then in my thoughts, I told God I didn't know where to look—I was ready to give up.

In the next moment, a message came into my head sort of like the phrase "punch biopsy" had. But this time I could FEEL it entering my head. In neither case was it an audible voice—if I had heard an audible voice, sitting there in the dark, I probably would have screamed and had a heart attack! But it was definitely not my thought. The message was, "Go look in the attic."

Well, I wasn't going to ignore THAT, so I went. I found something related and even more important, something life-changing, but the nature of the item will have to remain private.

*A Peace That Surpasses All Understanding*

Several years before that, I had the most surprising—and religious—experience of them all, another experience I never would have predicted in a million years. I was with a different group of people from any I have mentioned so far, but I had again been targeted for bullying. I think those of us who have been bullied or abused, until we heal, can project a vulnerability that makes bullies sense an easy target. This was low-level bullying, but had been going on for a while. On this occasion, the situation came to a head and turned on a dime.

The main and perhaps only true bully said something provocative to me. I don't recall what it was. But I clearly recall what happened next. I felt in my spirit that I should not defend myself in this case. I should do absolutely nothing and stand there and take it.

This reaction was mainly motivated by my own humility and sense of repentance: I knew that I wasn't 100% innocent, that I had played along, bantered back and forth, maybe said a few things in jest I shouldn't have. So at that moment, I felt like repenting for my part. *I'll just take my licks. I probably deserve this to some degree.*

For this to make sense, you need to know about the crucifixion of Christ. Maybe because I felt repentant rather than angry or fearful, I had a sensation of being stretched out on the cross, my arms spread wide, but I wasn't in agony, and I wasn't being punished. I was being STRENGTHENED! It was like I was on a supportive frame, like a scarecrow. And this experience gave me the strength to just stand there in COMPLETE PEACE! No stress hormones. No elevated heart rate. I just stood there, shocked by what I was experiencing.

As the whole room froze in silence to see how I would react, the momentum and the sympathy swung in my favor. After a couple more seconds of silence, the bully said, "How come everyone's looking at me like I'M the bad guy?"

One of the other guys piped up, "Because you ARE the bad guy."

The bully humorously jerked and said, "Oh!" The tension was broken, and the group continued on. Things were better after that. As I said before, sometimes you're called to just stand silent.

---

I want to repeat an important idea: I truly do respect you and your right to believe whatever you wish. I just wanted to present this section to you, as a gift of myself to you. That's the best thing that any of us can give to one another. Each of us is unique, and I wish for you new insight about how special you are, your gifts and talents, and your next steps to greatness here on Earth, in whatever time you have left. And now I'll close this section with the sign-off I use in my podcasts: Love ya guys!

# Final Thoughts

### *Promoting Functional Medicine/Holistic Health*

Healthcare cost-sharing programs such as Samaritan Ministries can serve as an economical alternative to health insurance, or just provide reimbursement for cash-pay functional services. This wonderful organization is one reason I'm alive today, and I've been recommending it for more than 10 years. Their referral program offers members a credit toward a monthly share when referred newcomers join. So if you sign up, please include "Happiness Reclaimed by Carol Diane" in the "how you heard about us" section.

We can support organizations that promote functional medicine such as the Institute for Functional Medicine and Rupa Health.

*Preventing and Ending Abuse*

"Domestic violence" includes physical, sexual, psychological, and financial abuse, plus sex trafficking and more. If you need help or wish to volunteer, visit the National Domestic Violence Hotline at www.TheHotline.org as well as the Rape, Abuse, and Incest National Network (RAINN), at centers.rainn.org.

*Our Potential Agreements*

Which points are currently igniting YOUR personal growth?

1. **Fresh Vision:** We're taking a fresh look at our problems, seeing a path beyond, and breaking old chains: "No! We're not doing this anymore!"
2. **Taking One Step:** We turn desire into success by starting with just one simple change.
3. **Perseverance:** We keep walking down this new road, step by step. We don't hand anyone the power to discourage us, but we heed wise warnings. We hold onto ANY blessing with an attitude of gratitude and let that sustain us for now.
4. **Freedom of Thought:** We exercise our right and responsibility to think for ourselves and give others that same respect.
5. **The Ripple Effect:** We are people who make a difference, as one life touches a life that touches a life that touches a life: We build trust by keeping our word and being transparent and authentic. We work to be precise, thorough, and judicious in our speech. We practice self-sacrifice. We recognize our potential to turn the world upside down!
6. **Transformation:** We are now freed from perfectionism and self-condemnation. We see our tremendous worth as children of God along with our wounds and shortcomings.

Only the full truth sets us free. We listen for "that still small voice" and allow God's Word to transform us.

7. **The Healthy Middle:** We strive for the healthy middle for all of life's choices.

8. **Empathy:** We work to understand and accept the feelings of others. We don't always agree, but we take time to see how they see it and feel how they feel it. THEIR feelings are as important as ours.

9. **Conflict Management:** We take "the plank" out of our own eye and purify our hearts as we learn conflict resolution skills. We seek the best for everyone, endeavoring to lovingly influence but not control: We leave room for God to work. We're on a path to greater closeness and REAL peace.

10. **Forgiveness:** We see with new eyes, piece the story together, and gain greater understanding, while also accepting that some things will never make sense here on Earth. We demolish the lie that forgiveness means enabling, condoning, or forgetting. Forgiveness limits the power of evil and removes the poison that will kill us.

11. **Taking Every Thought Captive:** We work to dwell on things that are lovely, admirable, or praiseworthy. We learn from the past and try to recognize evil when it confronts us today, but we refuse to stay stuck in the past or obsess about the future. Our battlefield is in our own minds, and we cling to the power of the Word as our weapon.

12. **Effective Parenting:** We offer guidance in a loving and positive way, while knowing we're capable of mistakes. We realize kids will test our boundaries but we stand strong to help them accept "no." We respect one another and stand united for the sake of our children.

13. **Financial Maturity:** We take responsibility for stewarding our funds wisely, which helps the entire family practice gratitude, contentment, generosity, sharing, and self-sacrifice.

14. **Appreciating Life:** We seek to treasure every moment, slowing down and being fully present.

15. **High-Quality Healthcare:** We ask that ALL doctors promote healthy habits, gain up-to-date knowledge of both research and clinical experience in their specialty worldwide, and be freed to devote more time to each patient.

16. **Holistic Health:** We advocate for optimal health for everyone through healthy habits and natural solutions using the biological truth that has existed for thousands of years. The power rests with us, the consumers! We live out the truth that the mind, body, and spirit are amazingly interconnected.

## *Until We Meet Again*

I hope we can unite around some of those agreements and work together to change the world! On my website, you'll discover the Powerful Strategies to help you create instant change.

I imagine we can all agree this book has been hard-hitting. Maybe these are the two questions we now must answer:

1. **Will we solve problems or just keep ignoring or attacking the messenger?**
2. **Are we ready to courageously follow our individual call to greatness?**

Let's turn this world upside down—starting with YOUR WORLD! And don't forget—any improvement you make will impact the whole world eventually. I'm sure of it.

**Nothing would bring me more pleasure than to hear about your progress!**

So here is one more idea for you as we end our communication for now:

> "Maybe your path is harder because you are called to something greater."

Please remember that when life gets hard. Let's move forward with love, patience, and endurance. We will each run our individual race until we hear that final praise: "…Well done, my good and faithful servant…" (Matthew 25:21 NLT).

Love ya guys!

# *Notes*

1. Maeda et al. Innate immunity in allergy. Allergy. 2019 Sep;74(9):1660-1674. doi: 10.1111/all.13788. Epub 2019 Apr 14. PMID: 30891811; PMCID: PMC6790574.
2. Science Direct. Chlordane. https://www.sciencedirect.com/topics/earth-and-planetary-sciences/chlordane Retrieved May 3, 2025.
3. United States Environmental Protection Agency. Volatile Organic Compounds' Impact on Indoor Air Quality. https://www.epa.gov/indoor-air-quality-iaq/volatile-organic-compounds-impact-indoor-air-quality Retrieved May 3, 2025.
4. United States Environmental Protection Agency. What Should I Know About Formaldehyde and Indoor Air Quality? https://www.epa.gov/indoor-air-quality-iaq/what-should-i-know-about-formaldehyde-and-indoor-air-quality Retrieved May 8, 2025.
5. Ziegler EE. Adverse effects of cow's milk in infants. Nestle Nutr Workshop Ser Pediatr Program. 2007;60:185-199. doi: 10.1159/000106369. PMID: 17664905.
6. Uher et al. Allopathic and Naturopathic Medicine and Their Objective Consideration of Congruent Pursuit. Evid Based Complement Alternat Med. 2020 Aug 6;2020:7525713. doi: 10.1155/2020/7525713. PMID: 32831878; PMCID: PMC7428928.
7. Greenan S. Rupa Health. How Functional Medicine Providers Look at "Optimal" Lab Ranges. https://www.rupahealth.com/post/how-functional-medicine-provider-look-at-optimal-lab-ranges Updated January 13, 2025. Retrieved May 5, 2025.
8. Ashcroft et al. (2024). Synthetic Endocrine Disruptors in Fragranced Products. Endocrines, 5(3), 366-381. https://doi.org/10.3390/endocrines5030027 August 15, 2024. Retrieved May 3, 2025.
9. Gangwisch et al. High glycemic index diet as a risk factor for depression: analyses from the Women's Health Initiative. Am J Clin Nutr. 2015 Aug;102(2):454-63. doi: 10.3945/ajcn.114.103846. Epub 2015 Jun 24. PMID: 26109579; PMCID: PMC4515860.
10. Taylor et al. A high-glycemic diet is associated with cerebral amyloid burden in cognitively normal older adults. Am J Clin Nutr. 2017 Dec;106(6):1463-1470. doi: 10.3945/ajcn.117.162263. Epub 2017 Oct 25. PMID: 29070566; PMCID: PMC5698843.
11. DiNicolantonio JJ, O'Keefe J. The Importance of Maintaining a Low Omega-6/Omega-3 Ratio for Reducing the Risk of Autoimmune Diseases, Asthma, and Allergies. Mo Med. 2021 Sep-Oct;118(5):453-459. PMID: 34658440; PMCID: PMC8504498.
12. Ravnskov et al. LDL-C does not cause cardiovascular disease: a comprehensive review of the current literature. Expert Rev Clin Pharmacol. 2018 Oct;11(10):959-970. doi: 10.1080/17512433.2018.1519391. Epub 2018 Oct 11. PMID: 30198808.

13. Ma et al. Excessive intake of sugar: An accomplice of inflammation. Front Immunol. 2022 Aug 31;13:988481. doi: 10.3389/fimmu.2022.988481. PMID: 36119103; PMCID: PMC9471313
14. Kearns et al. Sugar Industry and Coronary Heart Disease Research: A Historical Analysis of Internal Industry Documents. JAMA Intern Med. 2016 Nov 1;176(11):1680-1685. https://pmc.ncbi.nlm.nih.gov/articles/PMC5099084/
15. Nestle M. Food Industry Funding of Nutrition Research: The Relevance of History for Current Debates. JAMA Intern Med. 2016;176(11):1685–1686. doi:10.1001/jamainternmed.2016.5400
16. National Institutes of Health. Dietary Supplement Fact Sheet. Vitamin E Fact Sheet for Health Professionals. https://ods.od.nih.gov/factsheets/VitaminE-HealthProfessional/ Retrieved May 3, 2025.
17. Gyles C. Skeptical of medical science reports? Can Vet J. 2015 Oct;56(10):1011-2. PMID: 26483573; PMCID: PMC4572812.
18. National Library of Medicine. MedicinePlus. Drug-Induced Liver Injury. https://medlineplus.gov/ency/article/000226.htm Retrieved May 8, 2025.
19. KFF: McGough et al. Health System Tracker, How Has U.S. Spending on Healthcare Changed Over Time? December 20. 2024. https://www.healthsystemtracker.org/chart-collection/u-s-spending-healthcare-changed-time/#Total%20national%20health%20expenditures,%201970-2023 Retrieved May 3, 2025.
20. KFF: Cubanski et al. What Does the Federal Government Spend on Healthcare? February 24, 2025. https://www.kff.org/medicaid/issue-brief/what-does-the-federal-government-spend-on-health-care/ Retrieved May 3, 2025.
21. U.S. Department of Veteran Affairs. Whole Health Library. Estrogen Dominance. https://www.va.gov/WHOLEHEALTHLIBRARY/tools/estrogen-dominance.asp Retrieved May 3, 2025.
22. IARC Working Group on the Evaluation of Carcinogenic Risks to Humans, Hormonal Contraception and Post-menopausal Hormonal Therapy, IARC Monographs on the Evaluation of Carcinogenic Risks to Humans, No. 72, Lyon (FR): International Agency for Research on Cancer; 1999.
23. Kaneko et al. DICER1 deficit induces Alu RNA toxicity in age-related macular degeneration. Nature. 2011 Mar 17;471(7338):325-30. doi: 10.1038/nature09830. Epub 2011 Feb 6. PMID: 21297615; PMCID: PMC3077055.
24. Zhang et al. Alcohol Consumption and Age-related Macular Degeneration: A Systematic Review and Dose-response Meta-analysis. Curr Eye Res. 2021 Dec;46(12):1900-1907. doi: 10.1080/02713683.2021.1942070. Epub 2021 Jun 30. PMID: 34115943.
25. Vyawahare H, Shinde P. Age-Related Macular Degeneration: Epidemiology, Pathophysiology, Diagnosis, and Treatment. Cureus. 2022 Sep 26;14(9):e29583. doi: 10.7759/cureus.29583. PMID: 36312607; PMCID: PMC9595233.
26. American Cancer Society. All About Cancer. https://www.cancer.org/cancer.html#:~:text=In%20the%20United%20States%2C%201, answers%2C%20guidance%2C%20and%20support Retrieved May 5, 2025.

27. Jianhui et al. Global trends in incidence, death, burden and risk factors of early-onset cancer from 1990 to 2019: BMJ Oncology 2023;2:e000049.
28. Bartosch J. University of Chicago Medicine. Why Are More Young People Getting Cancer? What to Know as Cases Rise. https://www.uchicagomedicine.org/forefront/cancer-articles/why-are-young-people-getting-cancer Retrieved May 5, 2025.
29. IARC Monographs on the Identification of Carcinogenic Hazards to Humans. https://monographs.iarc.who.int/wp-content/uploads/2018/07/IARCMonographs-QA.pdf Retrieved May 5, 2025.
30. Donaldson MS. Nutrition and cancer: a review of the evidence for an anti-cancer diet. Nutr J. 2004 Oct 20;3:19. doi: 10.1186/1475-2891-3-19. PMID: 15496224; PMCID: PMC526387.
31. Shen et al. Evaluation of adverse effects/events of genetically modified food consumption: a systematic review of animal and human studies. Environ Sci Eur 34, 8 (2022). https://doi.org/10.1186/s12302-021-00578-9
32. Bawa AS, Anilakumar KR. Genetically modified foods: safety, risks and public concerns-a review. J Food Sci Technol. 2013 Dec;50(6):1035-46. doi: 10.1007/s13197-012-0899-1. Epub 2012 Dec 19. PMID: 24426015; PMCID: PMC3791249.
33. IARC. IARC Monographs Volume 112: evaluation of five organophosphate insecticides and herbicides, March 20, 2015. https://www.iarc.who.int/wpcontent/uploads/2018/07/MonographVolume112-1.pdf Retrieved May 5, 2025.
34. Brookes G. Farm income and production impacts from the use of genetically modified (GM) crop technology 1996-2020. GM Crops Food. 2022 Dec 31;13(1):171-195. doi: 10.1080/21645698.2022.2105626. PMID: 35983931; PMCID: PMC9397136.
35. Food & Water Watch. GMOs Plant Seeds For Corporate Control. March 2, 2021. https://www.foodandwaterwatch.org/2021/03/02/gmos-plant-seeds-corporate-control/ Retrieved May 8, 2025.
36. American Cancer Society. Cancer Facts & Figures 2025. https://www.cancer.org/content/dam/cancer-org/research/cancer-facts-and-statistics/annual-cancer-facts-and-figures/2025/2025-cancer-facts-and-figures-acs.pdf Retrieved May 5, 2025.
37. Ng KH, Rehani MM. X ray imaging goes digital. BMJ. 2006 Oct 14;333(7572):765-6. doi: 10.1136/bmj.38977.669769.2C. PMID: 17038712; PMCID: PMC1602038.
38. Ghisolfi et al. Ionizing radiation induces stemness in cancer cells. PLoS One. 2012;7(8):e43628. doi: 10.1371/journal.pone.0043628. Epub 2012 Aug 21. Erratum in: PLoS One. 2013;8(3). doi: 10.1371/annotation/15587a16-d9c2-446b-9601-924c2db5c5d9. PMID: 22928007; PMCID: PMC3424153.
39. Smith-Bindman et al. Radiation dose associated with common computed tomography examinations and the associated lifetime attributable risk of cancer. Arch Intern Med. 2009 Dec 14;169(22):2078-86. doi: 10.1001/archinternmed.2009.427. PMID: 20008690; PMCID: PMC4635397

Made in United States
Cleveland, OH
25 November 2025